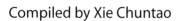

Compiled by Xie Chuntao

China Through the Ages

—from Confucius to Deng

(Vol. I)

新世界出版社
NEW WORLD PRESS

First Edition 2009

Compiled by Xie Chuntao
Translated by Zhou Gang, Li Yang and Wu An
Edited by Li Shujuan
Cover Design by Zhaoyuan Book Design Studio

ISBN 978-7-80228-565-1

Published by
NEW WORLD PRESS
24 Baiwanzhuang Street, Beijing 100037, China

Distributed by
NEW WORLD PRESS
24 Baiwanzhuang Street, Beijing 100037, China
Tel: 86-10-68995968
Fax: 86-10-68998705
Website: www.newworld-press.com
E-mail: frank@nwp.com.cn

Printed in the People's Republic of China

Preface

In recent years, China's reform and opening-up movement, as well as her rapid development, have increasingly drawn attention from foreign countries hoping for a deeper peek into what has always been a mysterious land for them. At the same time, China needs to reveal herself to the international community as much as possible, so as to integrate herself smoothly with the rest of the world.

However, rarely do we see books on China's evolution by local authors becoming popular with foreign readers, and there are even fewer widely-read books that cover Chinese history, culture, current situation and challenges. This is why I readily agreed when Mrs. Zhang Haiou, Deputy Chief Editor of New World Press, asked me to compile a book about Chinese history. I knew I would meet with many difficulties, but it would be worthwhile.

The idea for this book came from Mr. Lin Liangqi, former Deputy Chief Editor of China International Publishing Group. He has worked on media and cultural exchanges between China and the world, and is well experienced in this field. He proposed that the basic content of this book be centered on China in the past and present China. In his proposal, China's past would focus on the changes that have taken place in the country, her population and territory as well as her contributions to politics, economy and culture. Present China would mainly reflect China's independence, changing processes in foreign affairs, national unification—especially China's reform and opening-up—and the achievements related to her modernization. He also incorporated the suggestion of a senior journalist to name the book *China Through the Ages—from Confucius to Deng*, hoping to connect China's 5,000-year history with the two world-famous figures.

This book targets foreign readers knowing little about China and introduces Chinese history by telling typical stories in different eras. These stories can reflect Chinese territory evolution, national components, and origins of institutions, as well as Chinese ancient prosperity, modern weakness and today's rise. Chinese ideas, religions and way of act are exemplified by these stories, too. In one word, the goal of this book is to show foreign readers what China, Chinese people and Chinese culture are really like, and to enhance their knowledge and understanding of China.

The difficulties I encountered during compilation were quite beyond my estimation. The problems lay not only in the lack of knowledge my partners and I had about the reading habits of foreigners and the difficulties inherent in selecting stories from a 5,000-year-long history, but also in the dilemma of how to embody the essence of Chinese culture in these stories. Despite being exposed to Chinese culture for a long long time, I still find no simple way to summarize Chinese ways of thinking and behavior.

When this book was on the verge of being completed, the 8.0-magnitude earthquake hit Sichuan. China's humanitarian efforts and quake relief operations were unprecedented in their scale and magnificence. I was deeply moved and felt the necessity to ponder further about Chinese national traits and their connection with the outstanding attributes of the people in other nations of the world. This is why there may still be some flaws in this book, despite our best efforts. Given another chance in the future, and after hearing different opinions, we will definitely improve on it.

Thanks are due to Mr. Lin Liangqi whose ardent guidance on content and method benefited us a great deal. Mrs. Zhang Haiou and Mrs. Li Shujuan, Director of the English Department of New World Press, made important contributions to this book. My colleagues and partners Mr. Liu Yuebin, Mr. Zhang Jun, Mr. Li Qinggang and Mr. Shen Chuanliang did much of the compiling for this book, apart from their regular work. My sincere respect and gratitude to them all.

Xie Chuntao

May 20, 2008

Contents

Chapter 1

Prehistoric Legends and Mythologies

How did the world we live in come into existence? How was this universe created? How did human beings appear? Mankind had begun to explore these questions even during primeval times. People from different areas of the world offered different answers.

Christianity believed God created the world. Prometheus was the creator of man, in Greek mythology. People in ancient China also had their theories. The most popular one stated that the world was created by Pangu, and mankind was created by Nuwa. Several remarkable historic figures appeared one after another, teaching people life skills such as using fire, hunting and fishing, planting crops, building houses and treating diseases; there also appeared some who had management skills, and they organized people, fusing different tribes together through tribal wars, forming the rudiments of the Chinese nation.

1. Pangu Created the World

Long long ago, the whole world was just a big black ball of chaos. Inside this big egg lived Pangu, the earliest ancestor of the Chinese nation. He slept in this ball, grew and developed. Eighteen thousand years passed and Pangu suddenly woke up one day. When he opened his eyes, he was surrounded by darkness and couldn't see anything. He felt suppressed. So, with his broad, shining axe, he cracked the big ball open with all his might, and all the light (the good part of the ball) floated up, making up the blue heaven. All the cold and dark stuff stayed below, comprising the earth. The earth was finally separated from the heaven with clear air in between. Pangu was enormously relieved.

As the distance between the two was not that great, Pangu was afraid that the heaven and the earth would be joined again. So he stood on the earth and held up the heaven with his hands, trying to separate them further. Every day the sky rose ten feet, the earth became ten feet thicker and Pangu grew ten feet taller. Another 18,000 years passed and the distance between the heaven and the earth reached 90,000 *li* (45,000 kilometers). This is why the Chinese call heaven "*Jiu Chong Tian*". Pangu also became a giant, with a height of 90,000 *li*.

After his death, Pangu's left eye turned into the sun, and the right one into the moon. His limbs and body turned into the five big mountains.

Standing alone between the heaven and the earth, Pangu was the sole master of the world. When he was happy, the world would be clear and clean; when he got

angry, the skies would be overcast; when he took a breath, there would be a fierce wind; when he cried, there would be heavy rains; when his eyes twinkled, lightning would appear in the sky; and when he snored, there would be rolling thunder.

The sky was very high and the earth was dense after so many years; Pangu was extremely exhausted. His legs and arms were no longer powerful. He fell slowly and died. His left eye became the shining sun and the right one, the gentle moon. His body and limbs turned into five big mountains, and his blood formed the roaring waters. His veins became far-stretching roads and his muscles fertile land. The innumerable stars in the sky came from his hair and beard, and the flowers and trees from his skin and the fine hair on his body. His marrow and teeth turned into hard metals, round, shining pearls and smooth jade. His sweat turned into blessed rain and sweet dew that nurtured all things on earth.

Pangu was great. He had not only separated the heaven from the earth, but also created a beautiful world with his own body after he died. Pangu was thus lauded as a hero and ancestor by the Chinese nation.

The legend of Pangu was popular with the Han community. Other Chinese communities adopted similar versions of the legend, with different heroes.

Pangu created the world.

2. Nuwa Created Mankind

Pangu separated the heaven from the earth, and created natural landscapes that included wind, thunder, rain and various kinds of birds, animals, worms, fish, among others. But human beings, the rulers of the planet, had not appeared yet. Loneliness and desolation surrounded the whole world. Who created human beings? It was Nuwa, according to a popular legend.

Nuwa walked the desolate lands alone. No one talked to her. She felt lonely, and thought that something should be added to make the world more vital. She then crouched down beside a pool, grabbing some yellow soil and mixing it with water. Nuwa pinched the clay into a little creature resembling her own reflection in the pool.

She put the little thing onto the land, and the tiny thing came alive, screaming and dancing with great joy. Nuwa then named it "Ren" (human beings).

Though Ren's body was small, he was different from flying birds, crawling animals and swimming fish, as he was created by Nuwa with her own hands. Ren was full of wisdom and had a strong ability to manage all other creations in the world. Satisfied with what she had created, Nuwa was at peace. She

Nuwa

continued her work and humans were created one by one. There were now males and females, and all of them screamed and danced joyfully. Then they trooped away from her or ran, scattering in all directions. Nuwa could hear their laughter whenever she wanted. They were her children, and she didn't feel lonely any more.

Nuwa wanted to scatter these wise things across the earth, yet the vastness of the planet prevented her from achieving her goal even after much hard work. She was already exhausted. Then she came up with a new idea. She got a rope or a cane and put it in a pool. When the rope was filled with clay, she splashed it around, and people were formed. Nuwa was overjoyed at discovering such an easy way of creating people. She flung the rope around without stopping and the land was soon full of humans.

Nuwa was happy. But she was worried that if man was mortal, how would she create new batches? How could the human race

Nuwa used stones to mend the sky.

survive? She thought mankind should multiply by itself. Then she combined a man and a woman together to produce their own offspring and bear the responsibility to raise the next generation. Mankind began to breed and the population grew.

Nuwa has been called Gaomei, goddess of marriage or the earliest matchmarker, as she built the marriage system for mankind and brought men and women together. People offered sacrifices to Nuwa with a grand ceremony every spring, while young people joined together to play, dancing to wonderful music, trying to find their Mr. or Miss Right. So long as they loved each other, they could marry without any interference. Those who were married long but had no progeny also flocked to the temple, hoping that the goddess would bless them with a child.

Pangu created the world, and Nuwa created both humanity and the marriage system. People lived happily, with vigor and vitality, for many years. But the fire god Zhurong and the water god Gonggong had a great war for some unknown reasons. After his defeat, Gonggong butted the heavenly pillar Buzhou Mountain in the west, causing the sky in the northwest to collapse and the land in the southeast to be flooded. The sun, the moon, and almost all the stars moved to the northwest and the water and dust to the southeast. Another version says that all four heavenly pillars were knocked down, and the heaven and the land were split. A great fire raged and a fierce flood ravaged the land. Savage beasts and birds devoured and preyed on innocent people. Humanity was about to be destroyed.

Nuwa was extremely hurt by what had happened to her kids. She traveled to the four corners of the earth and picked up several red, yellow, blue, white and black stones to save her kids from the catastrophe. These stones were smelted with fire, and became a pasty liquid. Nuwa then used it to mend the cracks in the sky. She supported the four corners of the sky with the legs she had cut off from a giant turtle. Then she killed the black dragon in the Central Plains and drove the harmful beasts and birds away. Finally, she burned reeds and blocked the flood with the ashes. Mankind was saved by the great mother Nuwa and began to live a happy and tranquil life again. The only flaw was that the sky in the northwest and the earth in the southeast couldn't be restored. Both of them inclined slightly, so the sun, the moon and the stars fell down in the west while the rivers and oceans flowed to the northeast.

Different legends about the origin of humanity reflect those particular cultures' understanding of the world and themselves.

3. Three Sovereigns and Five Emperors

After the great mother Nuwa created human beings, they lived together in a totally natural way, threatened occasionally by natural disasters as well as natural enemies such as wolves, tigers and leopards. Mankind gradually evolved from barbarism to civilization, and some outstanding figures emerged over our long history.

There are different versions of the "three sage kings and five legendary emperors" legend (three sage kings: Fuxi, Suiren and Shennong or Tianhuang, Dihuang and Renhuang; five legendary emperors: Huangdi (the Yellow Emperor), Zhuanxu, Diku, Tang Yao and Yu Shun). Incidentally, unlike Greek mythology, China's myths always lack a clear pedigree. Gods often can not be distinguished from mortals, and sometimes the god is actually a man. For instance, it was said that Nuwa and Fuxi are the primogenitors of mankind. As legend goes, Nuwa married her brother, Fuxi. They

Fuxi and Nuwa, painting on silk, Tang Dynasty. Another legend relating to the origin of humanity goes like this: Fuxi married Nuwa, and they gave birth to human beings. In the painting Fuxi and Nuwa are both shaped like snakes with human heads, facing each other and with bodies tangled. Nuwa holds a pair of compasses, while Fuxi holds a carpenter's square, symbolizing the means of production and social order, respectively.

are both shaped like snakes, with human heads. Later they set up the marriage system, stipulating that brothers and sisters were not allowed to marry. This reflected the transition from consanguineous marriage to exogamy.

Although some haven't been listed within the three sage kings and five virtuous emperors, they made fairly great contributions to the development of mankind, therefore they were considered as the heroes in Chinese history.

Suiren (generally called "Suirenshi") was the inventor of fire-producing tools. At the time, people ate animal meat uncooked, as well as fresh plants and fruits. So Suiren taught people to rub wood together to produce fire and cook their food. Delicious food was then available to people and their general constitution greatly improved.

Fuxi (generally called "Fuxishi") was the inventor of hunting and the fish-net. He saw people pick up only the available plants and fruits, and they could never find food in colder seasons. Some

Suiren drilled wood to produce fire.

people even died of starvation. So he taught people to hunt, raise animals, make fish-net and use them for fishing. He also invented a way to make pottery, and taught people to cook food with it. Food varieties were greatly enriched. It was said that the influential Eight Diagrams was also invented by Fuxi.

Youchaoshi was the inventor of the house. He saw that people living in the wild were often attacked by animals. So he taught people to build houses with wood. The houses were built on stilts and even in trees as protection from wild animals.

Shennong (generally called "Shennongshi") was the inventor of agriculture and medicine. Although food variety was greatly enriched by collecting plants, fishing and hunting, sufficient food could never be secured. So Shennong taught people to cultivate crops and

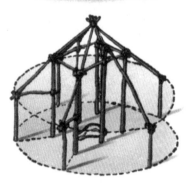

Houses lived in by primitive people

produce more grains with farm tools, including the plough and ploughshare. Shennong was saddened when he saw people threatened by diseases, and some even died young. He went around and tasted hundreds of herbs to discover materials for medicine. He also taught people to cure themselves. People's constitution was greatly

Shennong tasted hundreds of herbs.

Huangdi

improved and their lives were prolonged. Shennong governed the heavens in the south, and he was also the sun god. People in the south lived happy and harmonious lives under his governance.

Huangdi (the Yellow Emperor), the great emperor of heaven and the step-brother of Yandi in Chinese mythology, was generally regarded as the primo-genitor of all the tribes in the Central Plains. Huangdi practiced rule by virtue, and educated people in morality. He also developed farming and animal husbandry. Many inventions and production skills originated with Huangdi, such as the pestle, bows and arrows, ships and carts as well as well digging, taming cows and riding horses. His wife, Leizu, invented sericiculture, the raising of silkworms in order to produce silk. People could then wear beautiful clothes. Moreover, Cangjie, Huangdi's official historian, invented Chinese characters, and an official musician invented musical instruments. The tribe flourished and people lived in peace and harmony under his rule.

Chiyou, the leader of the Jiuli tribe in the south (it was said that he was the descendant of Yandi), was greatly covetous of Huangdi's throne. To gain widespread fame and prestige, Chiyou declared war on Yandi, his grandfather and heavenly god in the south. Yandi was defeated in present-day Zhuolu County, Hebei Province. The Yan tribe fled and joined the Huang tribe. Afterwards, the Yan and Huang tribes fought against the Chiyou tribe in a big battle, in present-day Zhuolu, south of Beijing. It was said that Chiyou's army was composed of 70 or 80 soldiers with bronze heads and iron foreheads, brave people from the Miao ethnic group, and fierce demons and monsters. Huangdi and Yandi's troops also included lots of ghosts, deities and beasts such as bears, leopards and tigers. A fierce battle ensued. Huangdi and Yandi finally won the war, Chiyou was killed and the uprising was suppressed. Everyone, including Chiyou's clansmen, lived a peaceful life and begat the next generation. That's why the Chinese call themselves "descendants of Yandi and Huangdi".

Yao, a tribal chief in the later era of patriarchal society, is well-known for his economy and his great concern for ordinary people. Yao is deeply venerated as a ruler of extraordinary virtue, humanity and kindness. He lived in a thatch hut, wore sackcloth and ate wild vegetable soup. People said that even the gatekeepers led a better life than Yao. Yao was beloved by all, and even his assistants were wise people.

A major incident occurred during Yao's reign. There were once ten suns in the sky. They were sons of Dijun, god of the eastern heaven, and lived in a tree called Fusang. They took turns every day to bring light and warmth to people. One day, the ten mischievous suns rose together, just for fun. Crops and trees began to wither, and many people starved. Savage beasts went out and attacked humans, who suffered terrible disasters. Yao then prayed to the god of heaven who sent Houyi, the best archer, flying to earth with his wife Chang'e, to save humanity by threatening the suns. The suns ignored the warnings of Houyi, who then shot down nine suns in a row. Yao remembered the benefits brought about by the sun. So he asked Houyi to leave one. Then Houyi shot the beasts and snakes threatening people's lives. Peace prevailed on the land.

Houyi had to stay on earth as the god of heaven was offended by what had happened. Chang'e was upset that they were now mortals and would die one day. Houyi went through all the difficulties, climbed the high Kunlun Mountain and asked the Queen Mother of the West to give him two divine pills. Houyi was told that taking one pill could make a person live long, and two could make a person become a god and ascend into the heaven. Houyi thought it would be wonderful to be immortal on earth, so he told Chang'e that they would eat the pills on a full moon night. Chang'e missed the life in the heaven and suspected that her husband had had a love affair with Luoshen. So she swallowed the elixir while Houyi was out hunting. Instead of flying back to heaven, Chang'e chose to live in the remote and desolate Moon Palace alone for ever, to avoid ridicule from other gods since she had betrayed her husband.

After being tribal leader for many years, Yao had to consider his successor. Yao was afraid that people would suffer if Danzhu became the leader, since the latter was not so skilled. So he tried hard to find a sage and bequeath his throne to him. Yao finally chose Shun after great effort.

Shun's father was Gusou, a blind man. Shun's mother died shortly after his birth. Gusou married another lady and had kids. The son was called Xiang.

Houyi shot all the suns down except one with his arrows.

Shun had always been good to his father, stepmother, stepsisters and stepbrother. But the arrogant stepmother and brother disliked Shun. Gusou also doted on his wife and younger son, and treated Shun badly. Though he was often abused by them, Shun was nothing less filial and

friendly to them. People were greatly
moved by Shun's virtue and devotion.
People offered their lands and fishing
grounds to others in places where Shun
worked; pottery was deemed attractive
and durable in the place where Shun
made it. People followed Shun wherever
he went. So the place where Shun lived
turned into a big town after several years.
The clan elders recommended Shun to
Yao for the former's filial piety and great
capabilities.

Yao was so keen on finding a
successor that he gave his two daughters,
Ehuang and Nuying, to Shun, along with
cows and sheep, and helped him mend his
granaries. Then Yao dispatched his nine

Shun

sons to live together with Shun to find out whether Shun was really
filial and talented.

Shun's stepmother, stepbrother and father were extremely
jealous of Shun's wealth and improved social status. They set a
trap for him. They pretended to repair the barn, and asked Shun for
help. Shun's two wives learned that they were villainous, and made
Shun wear clothes with bird-shaped patterns. When Shun climbed
to the top of the barn, his relatives pulled out the ladder and started
a big fire. Shun had no way out, screaming and flailing. Just then
he turned into a big bird and escaped.

Then his relatives came up with another idea, and asked Shun
to help drill a well. This time Ehuang and Nuying made him wear
dragon-shaped patterns with an old coat outside. They told Shun to
take off his clothes, should he be in danger. As Shun descended to

the bottom of the well, his relatives began to drop stones and lumps of earth in the well, attempting to bury him alive. Shun took off his clothes and turned into a dragon, diving deep and swimming to another well.

After hearing the reports from his sons and daughters, Yao thought Shun was indeed both filial and talented, thus he decided to give his throne to Shun. Yao tested Shun further and helped him gain experience by placing him at various posts. When Shun was well positioned to succeed, Yao held a ceremony and granted the throne to Shun. Shun, like Yao, lived in a very frugal way and showed great concern for his people by doing a lot of favorable and practical things. And instead of offering the throne to his son, Shun chose Yu, who made great contributions to flood control, as his successor when he was getting old.

Yu's father, Gun, was the leader of the Xia tribe during Yao's time, and was said to be the great grandson of Huangdi. According to the *Bible*, Jehovah unleashed floods upon the earth to punish humanity. Similarly, it rained heavily during Yao's later years as a ruler; rivers swelled up and overflowed everywhere. There was much suffering. Gun seemed to be a fairly competent tribal leader and was assigned by Yao to regulate the floods. Gun built dikes and dams to hold back the waters. But the waters soon overwhelmed the dams, and the floods returned. Gun failed to overcome the floods after nine years of effort. Yao (or Shun in other version) was offended and ordered Gun's execution. It was said that Gun's body lay there for three

Yu

years and did not decompose—and then Yu was born from Gun's belly.

Yu decided to carry on his father's unfulfilled task, and was assigned by Shun to control the flood. First he went to the east along the Yangtze River and to the north along the Yellow River, traveling across Huaihe River and Jishui River to research the territory. He then concluded that his father's failure could be attributed to the fact that just building dams to hold back water didn't work. Yu then formulated another plan to control the flood. As water flowed to a lower place, Yu cleared the stagnation, dredged the rivers and had new channels cut so that the water could flow safely and freely out to the sea. It took almost 13 years for Yu to quell the flood.

As legend goes, Yu was so busy controlling the water that he neglected his marriage. He got married at 30. He went back to the water-control construction site on the fourth day after his wedding. Yu passed by his house three times in 13 years but never went in. His story, a parable of morality, dedication and devotion, was passed down through generations.

Thus Shun asked Yu to take over the throne when he grew old.

Yao, Shun and Yu are sages according to ancient Chinese legend. Yu's son, Qi, ascended the throne after Yu's death and established the Xia Dynasty (*c.*2070-1600 BC), the first dynasty with a name in Chinese history.

All these legends reflect, to some extent, the ability of the earliest Chinese ancestors to adapt to nature, utilize natural resources and organize human society. Some of the legends also reflect the ideologies of the Chinese nation. For instance, when Yao chose Shun as his successor, he paid great attention to his morality, behavior and capability, indicating that a combination of morality and capability was most favored in choosing officials in ancient

China. Yu did whatever it took to bring the floods under control, regardless of his own family's well-being. This story also reflects that ordinary people want their officials to be selfless and devoted. All these thoughts and ideals are deeply rooted in the hearts of the Chinese, and still prevail in Chinese society today.

Chapter 2

Birth of the Chinese Civilization

China is renowned for its glorious civilization, evolving over thousands of years and remarkably different from that of other advanced nations. With respect to the country's origins, China also had its own unique early state system. The flowering of "a hundred schools of thought" during the Spring and Autumn Period (770-476 BC) was a sign that the Chinese civilization was entering the stage of maturity. Confucianism occupied an even more important position in Chinese history, having a profound impact on the country up until present day.

1. Stone Age

Anthropologists believe that the earliest humans appeared two to three million years ago, with ancient apes as predecessor. From the perspective of the history of social development, the main difference between human and ancient apes was in the manufacturing of tools. After researching the early tools—stoneware—archaeologists divided the history of human use of stoneware into Paleolithic Age and Neolithic Age. Paleolithic man used polished stoneware, which was rough and simple; Neolithic man used forged stoneware, which was fine and rich. Over 300 Paleolithic ruins have been discovered in China, showing different characteristics in the southern and the northern regions.

Paleolithic Age

Early Paleolithic man is also referred to as Ape-man, since he had many of the characteristics of ancient apes. Several ape-men have been discovered in China: Yuanmou Man, who lived about 1.7 million years ago—discovered in Yuanmou County of Yunnan Province in 1965; Lantian Man, from about 800 to 600 thousand years ago—found in Lantian County of Shaanxi Province; Peking Man—found on Longgu (Dragon Bone) Hill in Zhoukoudian of Fangshan District, Beijing, in the 1920s, with full skeleton fossils and up to 100,000 pieces of stoneware, including cutting utensils, scraping utensils, sharp-topped utensils; there were also a six-meter ash layer, which indicates that they knew how to use and preserve fire.

People call mid-Paleolithic human early Homo sapiens or Paleoanthropus, and there is a gap between

Stone tools unearthed from the An'gangxi Ancient Cultural Relics Site of the Eastern Han Dynasty

him and modern man. In China, they include: Maba Man—Maba Town, Qujiang County, Guangdong Province; Changyang Man—Changyang County in Hubei Province; Dingcun Man—Dingcun, Xiangfen County, Shanxi Province; and Xujiayao Man—Xujiayao, Yanggao County of Shanxi Province. The stoneware in these places is more complex and intricate than that of the early Paleolithic Age. It includes scraping utensils, stone balls, carving utensils, etc. Several tons of incomplete animal bones have been excavated, which proves that a developed form of hunting was being employed. These remains date back to a time between 100,000 and 200,000 years from today.

Incisor fossils of Yuanmou Man

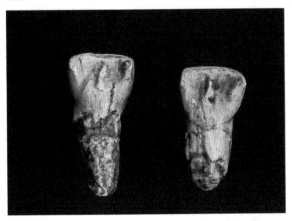

Late Paleolithic man is also known as late Homo sapiens or Neoanthropus Homo sapiens, who was roughly the same as modern man. As a result of geographical differences, they evolved into various races. Remains of Neoanthropus Homo sapiens have been found in China: Hetao Man—Wushen Banner of Inner Mongolia; Zhiyu Man—Zhiyu Village, Shuo County, Shanxi Province; Liujiang Man—Liujiang County, Guangxi Autonomous Region; Shandingdong Man (Upper Cave Man)—found in the caves on top of the Longgu Hill of Zhoukoudian, Fangshan District, Beijing. Neoanthropus Homo sapiens, represented by Upper Cave Man, date back to about 18,000 thousand years ago. They bear the characteristics of the yellow races. Their stoneware was fine and symmetrical, with sharp blades and decorative pieces such as beaded stones. The stone arrowheads indicate their use of bows and arrows, their polished stone sewing needles signified that they mastered sewing technology, and the flint stone is evidence of their artificial production of fire.

Paleolithic social organizations were characterized by bloods relations. They went on to develop into primitive communes, and then into clan communes. The heyday of clan communes appeared in the Neolithic Age.

Neolithic Age

Over 10,000 Neolithic remains have been discovered in China. Representative early Neolithic remains are: the Yuchanyan Relic Site in Daoxian County of Hunan Province, Xianrendong Relic Site in Wanxian County of Jiangxi Province, and Nanzhuangtou Relic Site in Xushui, Hebei Province, dating back to 10,000 years ago. Later discoveries include the Cishan Culture (found in Cishan, Wu'an County, Hebei Province) and the Peiligang Culture (found in Peiligang, Xinzheng City, Henan Province) 7,000-8,000 years old. The remains of agricultural crops and production tools in these places indicate that they had undergone the transition from hunting and gathering to early agriculture.

Middle and late Neolithic culture took on different archaeological landscapes due to the influence of various geographical

Stone arrow heads unearthed at Hulunboir, Inner Mongolia Autonomous

Yangshao Man lived in caves

environments and climate differences. It can be divided into several major areas of archaeological culture. These areas are, roughly, the Northern Part (the Great Wall area north and south of the Yanshan Mountains as its core); the Eastern Part (with Shandong Province as the center); the Central Plains (with Central Shaanxi, Southern Shanxi Province and Western Henan Province as the center); the South-eastern Part (with the areas around Taihu Lake as its center); the Southwestern Part (with the areas around Dongting Lake and the Sichuan Basin as its center); and the Southern Part (with the line from Poyang Lake to the Pearl River Delta as its central axis). Of these, the middle and late Neolithic culture of the Central Plains, the Northern Part, and the Eastern Part had a long accumulation of thought and other cultural riches, constituting the backbone of the Chinese pre-civilization. Its representatives are Middle Yangshao Culture, Hongshan Culture and the late Longshan Culture.

The Yangshao Culture was found in Yangshao Village of Mianchi County in Henan Province in 1921. Subsequently, similar archaeological sites in the Central Plains were all named this way.

Painted pottery—twin pots unearthed from the Yangshao Cultural Relics Site

Its culture existed 7,000-5,000 years ago, and its agriculture (chestnut growing), animal husbandry (pig and dog keeping), and pottery industry (with painted pottery) were considerably developed. The Banpo Ruins on the eastern outskirts of Xi'an represent the most complete preservation of a Yangshao Culture village, its architecture having the clear structure of overall arrangement.

The Hongshan Culture was so named after its discovery in the ruins behind the Red Hill of Chifeng City, Inner Mongolia. The same types of cultures are mainly distributed in southeastern Inner Mongolia, western Liaoning, and northern Hebei. It existed about 5,000 years ago. Exquisite jade ceremonial utensils have been unearthed, and altars and temples of gods and goddesses have been discovered, indicating that their society divided earlier and that it might have affected the culture of the Central Plains.

The Longshan Culture was found in Longshan Town, Zhangqiu County in Shandong Province in 1928. It is about 5,000 to 4,000 years old, and can be divided into the Shandong and Henan Longshan Cultures. The same type of cultural sites exist in the middle and lower reaches of the Yellow River. The remains of sheep, cattle, chickens and other livestock, as well as new varieties of farm tools, were found there. Black pottery (or eggshell pottery) was prevalent. The technology used in the processing of jade articles was advanced.

The middle and late Neolithic cultures in other regions of China also had their own characteristics. For instance, bronzeware appeared during the Qijia Culture (first discovered in Qijiaping, Guanghe County, Gansu Province) in the upper reaches of the Yellow River. Also discovered were altars and jade ceremonial utensils from the Liangzhu Culture (first discovered in Liangzhu, Yuhang County of Zhejiang Province) in the lower reaches of the Yangtze River. Moreover, the Neolithic culture of the northern grasslands was characterized by stoneware.

The stone cultures of the Central Plains, the northern and the eastern regions were the backbone of the development of Chinese civilization, although the latter originated from multiple sources.

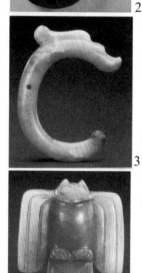

Jade articles unearthed from the Hongshan Cultural Relics Site: jade pig-dragon (1), C-shaped jade dragon (2-3), and jade bird (4)

2. Early States

Clay statue of a goddess unearthed from the Hong-shan Cultural Relics Site

The period of the early Chinese states were equivalent in developmental stage to the late Neolithic Age and the periods of the Five Legendary Emperors. These states already had massive, systematic manage-ment agencies. During Yao's time, he "arranged the responsibilities of various government officials systematically so as to achieve good results in every aspect". Later, Shun formally created the Si Kong, Si Tu, Shi, Gong, Zhi Zong, Dian Yue, Na Yan and other official positions. He attached great importance to the classification of various positions and the exercise of state management functions. Thus, by Yu's time, they had "reached the sea in the East and the deserts in the West". From the ancient historical records, we can see that social management functions in Yao-Shun-Yu era were prominently emphasized, but we can seldom find irreconcilable class contradictions therein. This is the critical stage when the early states of China formed. It can be said that China's early states were the social power organizations that formed at certain stages of social development and established over the various nations.

Mountain-shaped jade un-earthed from the Liangzhu Cultural Relics Site, dating back to 5,300-4,300 BC

The first Chinese states did not delimit their nationals with geographical regions. Long after China entered the era of civilization, the basis of society remained clans, rather than classification by geograph-ical regions. It was only after the vast social changes in the mid-term of the Warring States Period that the barriers of clans were broken, and registered house-holds became general social organizations.

The early Chinese states not only displayed repression and domination, but also had the conspicuous characteristic of mercy. Starting from the Xia Dynasty, there were penalties and prisons, and these remained the same in the Yin Dynasty (1300-1046 BC). There was a variety of characters for the word "penalty" on oracle bones. In the Yao and Shun eras, before the Xia (c.2070-1600 BC) and Shang (c.1600-1046 BC) dynasties, there were officials in charge of enforcing penalties and meting out punishments for violations.

However, the early Chinese states, based on a wide range of clan organizations, also possessed the function of managing and uniting the vast number of people in society, and showed mercy in the exercise of this function. Legend has it that Yao "promoted moral integrity, using it to build up goodwill toward his clan. Since the same race already lived in harmony, the merits of various officials (of the tribal union) were then identified." In Shun's era, although there were penalties, those for "mistakes arising from ignorance could be reduced or incrimination remitted," crimes due to inadvertent mistakes could be pardoned. *The Strategy of Gaotao, Shangshu (History of the Very Past)* recorded that Gaotao, who was in charge of penalties, advocated that "the emperor should understand his liegemen to stabilize morale," in order to practice virtue, and achieve harmony. Yu also advocated, "Be kind to the people in order to reassure them, who then will be submissive."

Between the Warring States Period (770-476 BC) and the Spring and Autumn Period (475-221 BC) , when Mo-tse summed up ancient politics, he said, "When the ancient sage kings practiced politics, they said, 'Do not let those who act without justice get rich, do not honor those who act without justice, and do not get close to those who act without justice'." "When the ancient sage kings practiced politics, they emphasized virtue and esteemed those with abilities." "The ancient sage kings elected dutiful sons to persuade people to serve their parents; they respected the virtuous who advised people to do good deeds; they promulgated decrees to instruct their people; they made clear rewards and punishments to reason with their people."

This shows that they primarily took righteousness and virtue into consideration in that era. Mo-tse said, "Therefore, the three previous generations of sage emperors were Yao, Shun, Yu, Tang, Emperor Wen and Emperor Wu of Zhou Dynasty (1046-771 BC)." It is obvious that the historical period when they esteemed righteousness and virtue was no other than the era of China's early states. At the end of the Warring States Period, based on his concept of historical evolution, Han Feizi believed, "They competed in ethics in the ancient times." This is in line with the prevailing sensibilities of the early nations in China, where they gave priority to mercy and ethics.

The famous statements in the book, the *Book of Rites*, concerning great harmony and well-being have been heard by educated people so many times that they know it by heart. Many people regard the two as different logos of the primitive era and a class-based society. In fact, the "xiao kang" (moderate prosperity) described in the *Book of Rites* was a reference to the social conditions after the formation of nations. However, is the "da tong" (great harmony) described in it a reflection of the primitive times before the existence of Chinese states?

It reads, "When the grand course was pursued, a public and common spirit ruled all under the sky; they chose men of talent, virtue, and ability; their words were sincere, and what they cultivated was harmony. Thus, men did not love their parents only, nor treat as children only their own sons. Competent provision was secured for the aged, employment for the able-bodied, and the means of nurture for the young. They showed kindness and compassion to widows, orphans, childless men, and those who were disabled by disease, so that they were all sufficiently maintained. Males had their proper work, and females had their homes. In this way (selfish) scheming was repressed. Robbers, filchers, and rebellious traitors did not show themselves, and people feel so safe that they don't even bother to close the door at night. This was (the period of) what we call the great harmony."

It is safe to say that the passage typically reveals China's primitive society. The concepts of "choosing men of talent, virtue, and ability; their words were sincere, and what they cultivated was harmony" and "common spirit ruled all under the sky" were the very reflection of both the social and administrative function of an early country. Coinciding with China's early times, "The Pursuit of the Grand Course" in the *Book of Rites* told about what the society of the Five Emperors' Period (*c.* 2600-2070 BC, beginning with Huangdi, the Yellow Emperor) looked like. We think that the line between "great harmony" and "moderate prosperity" was drawn to separate the Shun Period and the Yu Period—the division between the so-called "practice of the Grand Course" and the "eminent men of the three dynasties". It was not the watershed between a primitive society and a class-based society, but a boundary between a primitive country and a relatively developed country.

3. Confucius and His Doctrine

Confucius (551-479 BC) was born in Zou Yi, State of Lu (southeast of present-day Qufu City, Shandong Province). Legend holds that Confucius, a famous thinker, educationist, and the founder of the Confucian School in ancient China, had 3,000 followers, and 72 virtuous and talented disciples. He was said to have led his disciples on a journey to many states for 14 years. Confucius was traditionally credited with composing the *Spring and Autumn Annals*, editing the *Book of Songs* and *Book of History*, forewording the *Book of Changes*, and finalizing the *Rituals of Zhou* and *Book of Rites*. In short, Confucius's philosophy exerted far-reaching influence on the later ages.

Confucius was born in the State of Lu into an impoverished noble family. His father died when he was an infant. Although he was poor, at 15 he set his heart on learning. He was good at learning from others, saying: "Even when walking in a party of three I can always be certain of learning from those I am with. There will be good qualities that I can select for imitation and bad ones that will teach me what requires correction in myself." (Quoted from *Shu Er* of the *Analects of Confucius*) He followed no regular teachers, but he was so eager to learn and worked so hard that his fellow townsmen addressed him respectfully as "erudite". Confucius was firmly established at 30, when he began to teach students and give lectures. Some famous scholars and diplomats in history, such as Yan Lu, Zeng Dian, Zi Lu, Bo Niu, Ran You, Zi Gong and so forth, were his early followers. His initiative in setting up private schools broke away from the convention of learning in official schools and made instruction available to commoners. Thus, education was no longer regarded as a privilege monopolized by the nobility, but a right that an ordinary person was also entitled to and had access to.

From his 20s, Confucius was determined to take up an official career, so he showed great concern for state affairs,

Confucius

constantly making public comments on them. By 30, he enjoyed some reputation. When Duke Jing of Qi paid a formal visit to the State of Lu, he summoned Confucius to an interview out of admiration. They talked about Duke Mu of Qin, who was plotting to dominate the world at the time, and from

Disciples of Confucius

then on, Confucius kept in contact with Duke Jing. In the 25th year of Duke Zhao of Lu (517 BC), a civil war broke out in Lu. Duke Zhao was forced to flee the country for the State of Qi, and so was Confucius. When Confucius arrived in Qi, he was well received, and given excellent pay and living conditions. When Duke Jing of Qi consulted him on how to administrate a country, he answered, "A monarch behaves a monarch, an official behaves an official, a father behaves a father, and a son behaves a son." This meant that only by keeping a strict distinction between the upper class and the lower class, the noble and the humble, could society and family be put in order, organized and properly managed.

In the 27th year of Duke Zhao of Lu, some senior officials in Qi schemed to bring harm upon Confucius. On hearing the news, he turned to Duke Jing of Qi for help. Duke Jing said, "I am too old to be counted on for any help now." Confucius was compelled to take flight to Lu in a hurry, where he retired to a life of "sorting out historical documents and compiling and writing books". His disciples grew in number, and people came from distant states to become his disciples.

At the time, political power in Lu was in the hands of a Mr. Ji, who was controlled by his steward Yang Huo. Confucius was disappointed with the situation as it was—in his words, he would not have "assistant officials seizing the main power of the state"—and was reluctant to seek public office. He said, "Wealth and rank would be nothing but drifting clouds to me if I could not cultivate myself into a righteous man."

Confucius was not assigned to any post until Yang Huo was evicted in the 9th year of Duke Ding of Lu (501 BC). That year, at the age of 51, he was appointed as Zai of Zhongdu (the head of Zhongdu County). Because of his achievements in his one-year official career in Zhongdu, he was promoted to Sikong (a higher official position than Zai) and then to Great Sikou (an even higher position than Sikong). In the 12th year of Duke Ding of Lu, Confucius demolished the Three Huans' castles to weaken them (the Three Huans—Mr. Jisun, Mr. Shusun, and Mr. Mengsun—were so addressed because they were the grandsons of Duke Huan of Lu, who wielded the political power of Lu). Not long after, the action was left unfinished, but the conflict between them was out in the open.

Confucius left the State of Lu for the State of Wei. Duke Ling of Wei went out to the suburbs to meet Confucius.

In the 13th year of Duke Ding of Lu, the State of Qi sent 80 beautiful women to the State of Lu. Mr. Jihuan accepted them and was immediately infatuated with their singing and dancing, subsequently paying little heed to court affairs. Confucius

lost hope. Then, in the memorial ceremony of Lu in the suburb of the capital that year, the ruler did not give Confucius the sacrificial meat that was usually assigned to the officials. Confucius knew what Mr. Ji meant: he did not want him any more. So Confucius had to leave Lu to find a way out in other states, and thus commenced his travels to many countries—at the age of 55.

Confucius met Duke Jing of Qi.

Confucius went to the State of Wei first, where Duke Ling showed respect to him instantly and conferred 300,000 kilograms of grain on him as salary. But Duke Ling did not appoint him to any official post, nor did he allow him to partici-pate in political affairs. Confucius stayed in Wei for about 10 months, and after some people slandered him before Duke Ling, the Duke became suspicious of him and appointed some men to keep watch on him. Confucius had to leave Wei with his disciples. He planned to go to Chen, but when he passed by the city of Kuang, he was hemmed in there by mistake for five days. He had a hard time getting away from Kuang and reaching Pu, where he ran into armed rebellion led by the aristo-crat of Wei, Mr. Gongsun. He was besieged again. After freeing himself for a second time, Confucius returned to the State of Wei. Duke Ling of Wei was pleased and went out of the city to welcome him in person. After that, Confucius left Wei and returned several times, partly because Duke Ling of Wei treated him well, partly because Confucius had nowhere to go.

When he was 59, Confucius left the State of Wei for the State of Chen, through Cao, Song, and Zheng. He lived in Chen for three years until Wu invaded Chen. He had to move again to avoid the turmoil and chaos of the war. When the people of Chu heard the news that Confucius had arrived at the boundary between Chen and Cai, they went to meet him. However, the officials of both Chen and Cai were fully aware that Confucius held strong objections to what they had done. They feared that Confucius would be put in an important position and dispatched their men to besiege Confucius and his disciples on the way. There were neither villages nor inns to accommodate the group, and they soon ran out of food. They had nothing to eat for seven days. In the end, they only narrowly escaped death because Zi Gong came to rescue with the soldiers of Chu. Confucius returned to Wei at the age of 64.

Confucius served the Duke of Lu at a banquet.

With the help of his disciple Ran Qiu, he was ushered into Lu at the age of 68, held in high esteem but not in an official position as before. In the 16th year of Duke Ai of Lu, Confucius died of illness, at the age of 73.

The ruling class kept respectfully aloof from Confucius, holding him at arm's length. In fact, Confucius only had a hand in politics for about four years, which he made good use of and for which he was promoted rapidly. However, due to his political disagreements with the authorities, he had to part ways with them. Confucius devoted his later years to sorting out historical documents and propagating his doctrine.

Throughout his life, Confucius threw his whole being into setting up a systematic theory of Benevolence, which studies the relationship between people based on feudal ethics. The theory of Benevolence was a development and elaboration of primitive humanity. He advocated exemption from punishment, lessening

Confucius was surrounded by enemies in the State of Chen.

taxes and levies to lighten the burden on people, and opposing excessive exploitation and oppression. He attacked despotic rule, proposing to "encourage frugality so as to cherish people and lay tasks on them when the time comes". With respect to the administration of the country, he argued in favor of "*shu, fu, jiao*", namely, to multiply, enrich, and educate the people. The argument made up an important part of his political theory as well as his ideology of Benevolence.

Confucius laid special stress on selecting talented people for official posts, insisting that the only criterion used for choosing a person be his virtue and ability. He said, "The accomplished scholar is not a utensil," requiring that a person be versatile in order to meet the various needs of the society.

Confucius was consistent for decades in committing himself to education, and he was "the No.1 educationist of China". He set up private schools in the capacity of an individual and broke free from the convention of "going to school at official ones". Conse-

His disciples held a funeral for Confucius.

quently, education was no longer a patented right availed only by the ruling class—a remarkable achievement in history. He put forward the clarion call that "every one is entitled to education." Most of his students were commoners, and children of the rich and powerful made up only a small fraction. Being fully aware of

Offering sacrifices to Confucius

the significance of education, Confucius lived up to his words: he never wearied of teaching others what he learnt. His goal in education, closely linked to polity, was definite: to cultivate new talents for a harmonious society and the beneficent government he longed for. His belief that "those who were properly educated held the reins of government" broke the hereditary and aristocratic monopoly of the official posts.

With regard to political character, moral accomplishment, and adherence to principle, he cherished the political ambition and goal of remolding society. He sought public office because of this goal; however, he often ran into snags and was foiled everywhere, because he did not hanker after high positions and handsome salaries, and never renounced his principles and ideals. He once said, "Wealth and rank would be nothing but drifting clouds to me if I could not cultivate myself into a righteous man." He kept his words with his lifetime struggle, which explains why people of later generations have deep respect and admiration for him.

Confucius's thought is a valuable spiritual treasure for both China and humankind. The essence of Confucian theory will continue to play a positive role today.

Chapter 3

Formation of a Unified Country

Successive Chinese feudal dynasties dreamed of establishing a unified empire. From the first centralized feudal empire set up by Emperor Qin Shi Huang to the death of the last feudal empire, China's history has seen the Qin (221-206 BC), Han (206 BC-AD 220), Sui (581-618), Tang (618-907), Yuan (1271-1368), Ming (1368-1644), and Qing (1644-1911) empires, all of which achieved prosperity and unification. Although there were also such split periods during the Southern and Northern Dynasties (420-581), Five Dynasties and Ten Kingdoms (907-965), as well as confrontation between the Song (960-1279) and Jin (1115-1234) dynasties, they lasted for relatively short periods.

1. How Emperor Qin Shi Huang Unified China

Although the Xia (*c*.2070-1600 BC), Shang (*c*.1600-1046 BC), and Zhou (1046-221 BC) dynasties existed before Emperor Qin unified China, they were not unified, centralized empires in the true sense, considering their national form, political structure and social economy. The formation of the Chinese empire originated from Emperor Qin Shi Huang, the first emperor in Chinese history. The 2,000-year-old feudal system introduced by Emperor Qin Shi Huang was followed till the Qing Dynasty (1644-1911).

Emperor Qin Shi Huang, born as Ying Zheng, was the son of Zhuang Xiangwang, king of the State of Qin. He succeeded his father's regality at 13 and took the helm at 39. The State of Qin

Emperor Qin Shi Huang

was in full development during the late Warring States Period (475-221 BC). The state power naturally fell into the hands of Prime Minister Lü Buwei when Emperor Qin ascended the throne. In the year 238 BC, Emperor Qin assumed control of state affairs and immediately erased the power of Lü Buwei. He then appointed Wei Liao and Li Si as part of his cabinet. After defeating the other six states—Han, Zhao, Wei, Yan, Chu and Qi—through alienation and Machiavellian diplomacy between 230 BC and 221 BC, Emperor Qin finally built the Qin Dynasty, the first unified, multi-national and centralized country in Chinese history.

The establishment of a highly

centralized state by Emperor Qin after the unification of the six states was an unprecedented measure. The previous national organs based on feudal separation could not follow the latest development, so Emperor Qin identified measures to adjust, improve and strengthen the centralization rule after unifying China.

First, changing the title of "king" to "huang di" (emperor). The supreme rulers in the Spring and Autumn Period (770-476 BC) and Warring States Period (475-221 BC) were generally called "king". But Qin Shi Huang considered his achievement superior to the legendary "san huang" (three emperors) and "wu di" (five emperors). As the title of "king" would never distinguish him from other rulers, Qin Shi Huang ordered his ministers to discuss possible titles for him. After due consultation, all the ministers held that out of "tianhuang", "dihuang" and "taihuang" in ancient China, "taihuang" was the most distinguished. But Emperor Qin Shi Huang was still not satisfied, and created a new title for himself: "huang di": "Huang" from "taihuang" and "di" means "emperor". "Huang di" replaced "king" and became a new title for supreme rulers from then on. Qin Shi Huang also became the first emperor of China.

Then Qin Shi Huang decreed that title conferring would be abolished, and so an emperor would not be allowed to confer a title on the previous emperor. Emperor Qin Shi Huang also proclaimed himself "shi huang di", "shi" meaning "first". He hoped that his descendants would follow in his footsteps to rule China for eternity. They would be known as "2nd generation of emperor", "3rd generation of emperor", and so on until infinity. In order to show the power and distinction of the emperor, a series of systems was set up in the Qin Dynasty. An emperor's name was not allowed to be mentioned in words. An emperor called himself "zhen", his seal "xi", while these two words were forbidden to be used by the common people.

Second, executive organizations in central government were systematically reorganized. The central power of the Qin Dynasty was an extension and expansion of the State of Qin. But the names of the official positions and the actual powers were changed: the supreme ruler was emperor, and *Chengxiang* (Prime Minister), *Taiwei* (Great Commander) and *Yushi Dafu* (Censor-in-Chief) were the three most important posts besides the emperor. *Xiang, Xiangguo*—official posts of the State of Qin in the Warring States Period—were changed to *Chengxiang* (Prime Minister) in the Qin Dynasty. Li Si was appointed the first Prime Minister, serving as the chief of hundreds of officials. *Taiwei* (Great Commander), the top official governing military affairs, was originally called *Wei, Guowei* and then *Taiwei*. The Qin Dynasty originally had the post of *Yushi*. And the newly added *Yushi Dafu* (Censor-in-Chief) was designated to supervise and check related things; he was only next to the Prime Minister in power. There were nine cabinet ministers below the "three dukes". The actual number exceeded nine, and most of them originated from the State of Qin with a few newly established posts.

One important characteristic of the centralized power system during the reign of Emperor Qin was that the emperor arrogated both military and political powers. To avoid power passing into

Model of a terra-cotta warrior and horse, unearthed from the No.2 Pit of Qin Shi Huang's mausoleum in Lintong, Shaanxi Province, in 1976

others' hands, the Prime Minister, Great Commander, Censor-in-Chief were created to govern political, military and supervisory matters without interaction. The Prime Minister led court discussions while helping the emperor in his daily affairs, and acting as sounding board for him. Military power belonged to the Great Commander. The Censor-in-Chief also helped make sound suggestions. Although he was seemingly the top military official, the Great Commander only had the right to train soldiers, and no right to transfer troops. Since the three dukes did not report to each other, the emperor still had the final say in everything.

Third, the local political organs were restructured. Four administrative organs were set as

Model of a bronze chariot unearthed from the No.2 Pit of Qin Shi Huang's tomb

follows: prefectures, counties, townships and rings.

The feudal bureaucratic system introduced by the Qin Dynasty represented a great improvement in China's political system. It changed the hereditary system and abolished the vassal system. Each official was paid under relevant regulations. His salary varied, depending on his rank. This system was implemented nationwide after Qin unified China and continued for over 2,000 years.

Besides the establishment of the emperor system and centralization of political power, Qin Shi Huang was also responsible for a few economic and cultural unifications.

An order to protect feudal land ownership was issued. According to an order introduced in the 31st year of the Qin Dynasty (216 BC), landowners and yeomen were required to report the size of their lands to the state. This meant that their ownership were recognized and protected by the government. The state also issued a policy that emphasized agriculture while restraining commerce, to fight against non-productive activities and encourage people to take part in agricultural and cottage industry. This measure actually protected feudal land ownership and developed a feudal economy.

The currency, measures and weights were standardized. Before unification, the currency's varied shapes, sizes, weights and units made it extremely complex. After Qin unified China, Emperor Qin Shi Huang ordered that the currency be standardized nationwide, with gold as the upper currency and "Yi" as the unit; a round coin with a square hole (*Ban Liang* Coin) would be used henceforth. At last, this round coin continued to be used for more than 2,000 years.

Measuring apparatus dating from the Qin Dynasty

The measures in use were also complicated. The Qin Dynasty had already identified unified regulations about measures during the Reform of Shang Yang. The measures were standardized based on the original Qin measures, after unification. The government also carved the rescript in the government-made metrology and sent out nationwide as standardizations.

The Warring States Period was defined by different languages and characters, holding back the

Half-*liang* coins of the State of Qin, and a mold

development of cultural exchanges. Emperor Qin Shi Huang standardized the written characters, making the Qinzhuan the standard font in 221 BC. Based on the theory of the five cyclic virtues of *Yin-Yang* masters in the Warring States Period, clothes and banners or flags adorned with feathers were black, and the systems of commander's tally, beretta, and carriage shall base on number six under relevant regulations. Emperor Qin Shi Huang even ordered the burning of the *Book of Songs*, the *Book of History* and articles from various schools, and the burial of over 400 Confucian scholars alive caused by the flee of Hou Sheng and some other people he sent to seek for medicine of eternity.

Emperor Qin Shi Huang ordered the burning of most previously written books, and the burying alive of Confucian scholars.

Several kings in the Warring States Period had built strongholds and bastions of different sizes, affecting normal transportation. So Qin Shi Huang ordered that these buildings be removed. A road was built in 220 BC, with the capital, Xianyang, at the center. Then another straight road from Xianyang, stretching to the north, was built in 212 BC. It took only two years to finish the project. All the new roads in what is today's Hunan, Jiangxi, Guangdong, and Guangxi provinces formed an easy and convenient transportation network, with Xianyang at its center. Once the width of the roads and that of the carriage wheels were standardized, transportation became even easier.

Qin Shi Huang sent General

Meng Tian to fight the north nomadic Huns, in an effort to defend the empire. Meng Tian defeated the Huns in 214 BC and took back the Hetao Area (at the top of the Great Bend of the Yellow River in present-day Inner Mongolia and Ningxia). The government then built towns and stockade villages, and moved people there in a bid to solidify frontier defenses. Then Qin Shi Huang conscripted farmers to build a wall from Linyao, Longxi in the west and Liaodong (region to the east of the Liaohe River, namely eastern and southern part of present Liaoning Province) in the east to protect themselves from the Huns. That was the origin of the world-renowned Great Wall. It prevented the northern nomadic tribes from entering, and secured a peaceful life for the labor force in the south.

The building of the Great Wall started in the Qin Dynasty.

Qin Shi Huang also sent troops to conquer the part of the Pearl River Basin inhabited by the Yue people. Counties such as Guilin, Nanhai and Xiangjun were established, and about 500,000 people were sent there from the central area to live with the Yue people. Qin Shi Huang assigned Shi Lu to build the Lingqu Canal to ease transportation. Its two channels exquisitely connected the Xiangjiang River (in the Yangtze River Basin) and the Lijiang River (in the Pearl River Basin). Located in Guangxi Zhuang Autonomous Region, the 30-kilometer Lingqu Canal, one of the world's oldest man-made canals, can still irrigate around 40,000 *mu* of land today.

These measures adopted after unification exerted profound effect on the empire, helping to eliminate feudal separation, strengthen centralized power, consolidate the unification of a multi-national country, and boost the feudal economy and culture.

Qin Shi Huang was an extremely influential figure in Chinese history. Taking his cues from history, he unified China and adopted a series of measures to cement and consolidate the country, bringing immense benefits to society. But heavy taxation, corvee and cruel punishment imposed on the people caused untold suffering, and the first large-scale peasant revolt in Chinese history broke out in the second year after Qin Shi Huang's death. The Qin Dynasty was overthrown.

2. Constant Separation and Unification

The Qin Dynasty existed for less than two decades, thanks to Emperor Qin's tyranny. China then witnessed the Western Han (206 BC-AD 25), Eastern Han (25-220), Three Kingdoms (220-280), Wei (220-265), Jin (265-420), Southern and Northern Dynasties (420-589), Sui (581-618), Tang (618-907), Song (960-1279), Yuan (1279-1368), Ming (1368-1644) and Qing (1644-1911) dynasties. Tibet officially became part of China during the Yuan Dynasty. China's territory was enlarged greatly during the prosperous and flourishing Western Han, Tang and Qing dynasties, laying a solid foundation for the vast present-day country that is China.

The Western Han (206 BC-AD 25) and the Eastern Han (25-220) dynasties were founded on the territorial layout of the Qin Dynasty. The political, economic and cultural centers were still located in the middle and lower reaches of the Yellow River (Chang'an was the capital of the Western Han Dynasty and Luoyang of the Eastern Han Dynasty), and the territorial scope extended and changed. The territory of the Western Han Dynasty was mainly extended during Emperor Wu's rule, stretching to the middle of Korean Peninsula to the northeast, Gansu Corridor and Western Regions in the northwest, Yunnan and Sichuan and northern Hainan Island in the southwest. The famous Silk Road was also built at this time, playing a vital role in strengthening the communications between China and Central Asia, West Asia and Europe.

The territorial scope was narrowed during the Eastern Han Dynasty, after attacks from the Huns of northern China.

Afterwards China entered a period of seperation, namely the Three Kingdoms, Western Jin Dynasty (265-316) and Eastern Jin Dynasty (317-420), and the Southern and Northern Dynasties (420-589). The territory of the Three Kingdoms was similar to that of the Eastern Han Dynasty. Wei (220-265), Shu (221-263), Wu (222-280) all extended their territory during the Three Kingdoms period. As the Western Jin Dynasty was built by unifying Wei, Shu, Wu together, its territory was basically the same as that of the Western and Eastern Han dynasties, and the Three Kingdoms period. Yang Jian unified China and established the Sui Dynasty (581-618), which only existed for 38 years. The territorial layout of the Sui Dynasty during its prime was smaller than that of the Western Jin Dynasty. Although Hetao Area and the southeastern Mongolian Plateau were included in the territory, the Sui Dynasty lost Liaodong, the western part of the Western Regions and large parts of Yunnan-Guizhou Plateau.

After the brief Sui Dynasty (581-618), China entered the period of the Tang Dynasty (618-907), another brilliantly flourishing dynasty that followed the Western Han Dynasty. The Zhenguan years(627-649) of the Tang Dynasty, in particular, far surpassed previous dynasties in terms of culture, economy, agriculture, commerce, handicraft and transportation. The Tang Dynasty was well known to people across the world at the time, and "Tang" even became a synonym for China. Even today foreigners call the Chinese "Tang people", the overseas area inhabited by the Chinese "The Tangs' Street" (China Town) and traditional Chinese clothes, "Tang clothing".

The early and late periods of the Tang Dynasty contrasted sharply in their development, as did its territorial layout. In its prime, it not only boasted the territories of the Qin and Han dynasties, but also stretched to the west bank of the Sea of Japan, Sakhalin Island and southwestern Korean Peninsula to the northeast, Baikal Lake and the upper reaches of Yenisei River in the north and southern Hainan Island in the south. In western China, the Tang Dynasty also unified and tightened its control over the Western Regions. The border extended to the sea and its spheres of influence reached the Caspian Sea.

The Tang Dynasty lost a great deal of its land after the turmoil of 755, especially in its northeastern areas and Western Regions. The country suffered from chaos created by the warlords of the late Tang Dynasty. The period was called Five Dynasties and Ten Kingdoms (902-979), and lasted 54 years. Then followed the Liao Dynasty (916-1125), Song Dynasty (960-1279), Jin Dynasty (1115-1234) and so on.

Genghis Khan established the Mongol Khanate in the early 13th century. The Mongolian regime identified the state name as Yuan in 1271 and unified the whole of China in 1279. A unified central government was established and Tibet became an administrative region under the direct control of China's Yuan Dynasty.

The territory of the Yuan Dynasty (1279-1368) even crossed Eurasia, stretching to the Sea of Japan in the northeast, present-day Siberia Arctic Circle in the north, Wokuotai's (the third son of Genghis Khan) State (in today's Xinjiang), Chahetai's (the third son of Genghis Khan) State (in today's Xinjiang), Qinchahan's State (established by Badu, grandson of Genghis Khan, in today's Russia) and Yilihan State (established by Xuliewu, grandson of Genghis Khan, in today's Iran) and Nepal, India, Burma, Vietnam in the southeast. Tibet enjoyed a growing alliance with the Central Plain regions, politically, economically and culturally, especially after, Princess Wencheng of the Tang Dynasty entered Tibet. The Yuan Dynasty authorized the Sakya leaders to govern Tibet and directly participated in the identification of the officials, registered permanent residence, and taxation issues. Tibet then became a part of China. The Yuan Dynasty also possessed the largest territory in China's history.

The territory of the early Ming Dynasty (1368-1644) was similar to that of the late Yuan Dynasty: It bordered Korea along the Yalu River in the northeast. In the north, some northern Mongolian tribes were vassal states of the Yuan Dynasty. West of Hami, it bordered on Yilibali (evolved from the State of Chahetai) in the northwest. By the late Ming Dynasty, it bordered on the Ming territory along the Great Wall from Jiayu Pass in the west to Shanhai Pass in the east. The territory drew back to the Liaohe River Basin in the northeast; kingdoms were established by various Mongolian tribes in the northwest; Its borderlines were also pushed eastward in the western part of Yunnan. Macao and Taiwan were invaded by western countries during the late Ming Dynasty.

After the establishment of the Ming Dynasty, the government adopted a general closure policy toward Tibet. Religious leaders of local sections with political strength were conferred the titles of "Wang", "Fa Wang", "Guanding Guoshi"; inheritance of the throne of the "wang" was subject to approval by the emperor, and special envoys were sent to name the successors. Following what the Yuan Dynasty had done to Tibet, the Ming Dynasty set up the Dbusgtsang and Dokham Military Commissions, and the Olisi Prefecture of the Governor General to be in charge of the military and administrative affairs of Anterior and Ulterior Tibet, Chamdo and Ngari.

The late Jin, established by the Jurchens, grew stronger during the late Ming Dynasty and finally changed the nation's name to Qing. The central government adopted more severe governance toward Tibet in the Qing Dynasty, systematizing and legalizing ways to exercise its sovereignty over Tibet. The golden book and golden seal were bestowed by Emperor Shunzhi and the Fifth Dalai Lama came into power in 1653. The title of the Dalai Lama was officially confirmed then. Emperor Kangxi conferred the title of "Panchen Erdeni" on Lozang Yeshe, the Fifth Panchen Lama, and formally identified the name of the Panchen Lama in 1713.

Since then, the Dalai Lama in Lhasa ruled a large part of Tibet while Panchen Erdeni in Xigaze ruled other areas of Tibet. The Qing Dynasty established the grand resident minister in Tibet to supervise the local administration on behalf of the central government in 1727. The central authority also adjusted the administrative system to manage Tibet, abolished the monarchic (Jun Wang) system, set up the local government for Tibet (i.e. "Gasha"), providing for Tibet affairs to be governed by both the grand resident minister and the Dalai Lama in 1750. The central government in the Qing Dynasty created Twenty-Nine Regulations called "Regulations for Better Government in Tibet" concerning the post of grand resident minister in Tibet, the Dalai Lama, Panchen, reincarnation of living Buddhas, border defense, interactions with foreign countries, finance, taxation, monetary casting and management, and the support and management of temples. For over 100 years since then, the basic principles of the Twenty-Nine Regulations have always been regarded as norms for the administrative system and regulations in Tibet.

The Qing Dynasty finally fulfilled its historic mission of defining China's territory. Under the renowned Emperor Kangxi, the territory reached the sea in the east, Congling in the west, Zengmu Reef in the south, Outer Hingan Mountain Range in the north, Lake Balkhash in the northwest and Sakhalin Island in the northeast, covering a total area of 13 million square kilometers.

3. Initial Definition of the Chinese Territorial Layout

The Qing Dynasty established by Manchus finally fulfilled the historical task of defining China's territory. The territory of the Qing Dynasty stretched from Siberia in the north, Outer Hingan Mountain Range, north of Heilongjiang Province and Sakhalin Island in the northeast, Pacific Ocean in the east, Taiwan and its nearby Diaoyu Island and Chiweiyu in the southeast, islands near South China Sea in the south, Congling in the west and northern bank of Balekashichi in the northwest.

Several western countries invaded China in the middle of the 19th century and colonized it. They occupied China's territory in the following ways:

First, neighboring countries occupied Chinese territory. Russia, for instance, forced the Qing Dynasty to sign the Ey-Hwei Treaty in 1859, and the Sino-Russia Peking Treaty in 1860, seizing the areas in northern Heilongjiang Province and eastern Wusuli River. Russia also appropriated a great deal of land near Tangnu-wulianghai (Tuva), Kobdo, and the Lake Balkhash and the Pamirs area in the northwest by signing unequal treaties such as the Sino-Russia National Border in the Northwest Treaty in 1864 and Sino-Russia Treaty of Yili in 1881. After defeating China in the Sino-Japanese War, Japan also forced China to sign the Treaty of Shimonoseki, occupying China's Taiwan Province.

Second, superpowers from Europe made Chinese territories a part of the colonies they built around China. Britain and France were two typical examples. Britain brought the land from the Pamirs in the north to Yunnan, via Tibet, into its own colony while France got two chieftains, Diannan, Mengde to France-occupied Cochin China.

Third, western powers took over China's coastal areas forcefully. Macao was taken by Portugal, Hong Kong and Weihai by Britain, Jiaozhou Bay by Germany, Lushunkou and Dalian by Russia (later by Japan), Guangzhou Bay by France.

The Republic of China was founded in 1912. The new republic suffered greatly from severe border disputes in its early years, when Tsarist Russia in Outer Mongolia triggered "independent", "autonomous governance" incidents. Tangnuwulianghai was occupied by Russian troops in 1914. Moreover, Britain held the Simla Conference, aiming to take over Tibet. Representatives from the Chinese government refused to sign and recognize the so-called Simla Treaty.

The September 18 Incident broke out in 1931 and China's northeastern part was occupied by Japan. A war raged nationwide and China's northeastern, northern, eastern, southern, southwestern parts were all seized by Japan. The war came to an end in 1945 and China regained its lost lands—Taiwan Province occupied by Japan for 50 years, and islands near the South China Sea occupied by Japan during the Second World War. The territory of the new China stretched from the intersection point of Heilongjiang and the Wusuli Rivers in the east, The Pamirs in the west, Zengmu Reef in the south and Mohe in the north.

Chapter 4

Merging of Chinese Nationalities

The modern Chinese nation consists of the Han nationality, and 55 minorities. These peoples jointly created China's splendid civilization.

1. The Origin of the Han Nationality

As the world's biggest nationality, the Han nationality origi-nated from the middle and lower reaches of the Yellow River.

The Yandi and Huangdi tribes rose from the Central Plains, on the banks of the Yellow River, and formed an alliance. The two triggered the famous War of Banquan to decide the leader of the tribes. Huangdi achieved a decisive victory and dominated the Central Plains thereafter. Then the Xia, China's first nationality appeared, boasting a direct relation with the Huangdi tribe. The subsequent Zhou nationality was also related to the Huangdi and Yandi tribes in the Weishui Basin. Huangdi has been honored by the Han nationality as the ancestor, or "the original ancestor of humanity".

The Huangdi mausoleum or the legendary grave of Emperor Huangdi, a symbol of the origins of the Han nationality, was located on Qiaoshan Mountain covered with hundreds of ancient cypress, in Huangling County in the middle of Shaanxi Province. The Han nationality, originating from the Huaxia nationality, was not formed in a short period of time. It experienced three long and complex historical periods. Several tribes, including the Xia, Shang, Zhou, Chu, Yue, first developed into nationalities. Then the Huaxia nationality was formed after the Xia, Shang, Zhou, Chu, and Yue nationalities merged with part of the Man, Yi, and Rong nationalities. The Huaxia nationality was finally formed in the Han Dynasty (206 BC-AD 220).

1) The Rise of the Xia, Shang, Zhou, Chu, Yue Nationalities

The Han nationality actually sprang up from the develop-ment of the Xia, Shang, Zhou, Chu, Yue nationalities. The Xia nationality first rose in the middle reaches of the Yellow River and Luohe Basin between the 23rd century BC and 22nd century BC. According to the legend, before entering the Yellow River and Luohe basins, the Xia tribe was still primitive, governed by the clan commune system. Blood relations were the vital nexus between its members. Emperor Yu divided the tribe into nine prefectures, demonstrating that the Xia tribe had transformed its blood-based relations to geographical relations, and the Xia nationality was finally formed.

Due to imbalanced social development, while the Xia nationality evolved, the nomadic Shang tribe, located in the Shandong Peninsula, still regarded birds as totem and led a primitive life. However, with increased productivity, the Shang tribe also advanced; once subservient to the Xia Dynasty (*c.*2070-1600 BC), it now defeated the latter in a decisive battle and tribe leader Tang established a new slave country—the Shang Dynasty (*c.*1600-1046 BC). The Shang tribe evolved in to the Shang nationality and rose in the lower reaches of the Yellow River, transforming its blood-based relations to geographical relations.

The Zhou tribe, previously subordinate to the Shang Dynasty, lived in the Qin and Ju basins, upstream of Weishui River in Shaanxi and Gansu. History repeated itself once more. Like the Shang tribe, the Zhou tribe also transited from a primitive society to a class society; it established the Zhou Dynasty (1046-256 BC) by defeating the Shang Dynasty, which had defeated Emperor Jie of the Xia Dynasty. Then the Zhou nationality was formed. The Chu and Yue tribes also came to prominence and developed in the Yangtze River Basin, while the Xia, Shang and Zhou tribes mushroomed one after another in the Yellow River Basin. Compared with the Yellow River Basin, the Yangtze River Basin featured relatively slow development. All the clans and tribes in that area

Wuhuan Warriors on the March, from a mural in a Han tomb, Inner Mongolia Autonomous Region

were called "Man" (the barbarian) for a long time. And the "Man" in Jianghan area was called "Chujing".

The Yue nationality was actually initiated from the sudden rise of the Yuyues. The Baiyue nationality was scattered in a region that included present-day Jiangsu, Zhejiang, Guangdong, Guangxi provinces and the Yunnan-Guizhou Plateau. The nationality, with its different castes, lived together in a haphazard way, owing to imbalanced social development. Yuyue, one branch of the Baiyue nationality, (neighboring nationalities in the Central Plains of present-day Zhengjiang and Jiangsu provinces) embarked on the road to forming a nationality during the Shang and Zhou Dynasties, thanks to historical opportunity and its unique location. The establishment of the states of Wu and Yue indicated that Yuyue had come of age as well.

The rise of Xia, Shang, Zhou, Chu, Yue nationalities is

Xianbei warrior figurine unearthed from the Beiqi Tomb, Taiyuan, Shanxi Province

magnificent and splendid in the formation and development of ancient nationalities in China, representing the first stage of the formation of the Han Dynasty (206 BC-AD 220).

2) The Huaxia Nationality

These nationalities, like other aspects of Chinese history, continued to change and develop. Primitive tribes such as Xia, Shang, Zhou, Chu and Yue eventually developed into nationalities. Gradually these nationalities began to merge and their relations changed and developed greatly during the Spring and Autumn Period (770-476 BC) and Warring States Period (475-221 BC) by interaction, mutual penetration and assimilation, causing a trend of national integration.

The melding of nationalities in the Spring and Autumn Period first occurred among the Xia, Shang and Zhou nationalities. Parts

Mongolian warrior

Painting of King Wuling
of Zhao, mounted and in
barbarian attire

of Man, Yi, Rong, Di also merged during that period. The Huaxia
nationality was formed after the great coming together of nationalities in the Spring and Autumn Period. "Huaxia" then referred to a
new nationality—mainly composed of the Xia, Shang, Zhou and
Yi nationalities, as well as Man, Rong, and Di—in the Spring and
Autumn Period.

The nationalities merged smoothly and quickly in the Warring
States Period. In the south, the State of Chu, located in the Hanshui
and Yangtze basins, was witness to an increasingly advanced civilization and merging among various nationalities, after over 800
years of expansion and effective governance. The State of Yan
in the northeast also emerged as a powerful nation at the time.
Yan's general, Qin Kai, had once been taken hostage in Donghu.
Later, when he was home again, he led his army to a victory over
Donghu. The Yan territory expanded greatly. Yan's expansion in
the Liaohe River Basin defined ancient China's territory in the
northeast, and merged various nationalities in the basin into the

Huaxia nationality.

National integration is nothing but the collision of civilizations. The famous story of "Wearing Non-Han Uniforms and Cavalry in Battles" reflected how Chinese culture absorbed northern minority culture in the process of national integration. "Wearing Non-Han Uniforms and Using Cavalry in Battles" was a famous military reform launched by King Wuling of the State of Zhao during the late Warring States Period. King Wuling (during his reign between 325 BC and 299 BC), was the sixth King of Zhao, and he was determined to revitalize the State of Zhao. Although Zhao had a large army, its combat effectiveness was poor; it had heavy military equipment, and the long, wide uniforms restricted the soldiers' hands and feet, making them clumsy and inefficient. The north non-Han nationalities, however, wore short clothes and long trousers, and were agile from head to toe, riding horses and shooting arrows with ease. In addition, their bows and arrows were light, yet powerful, so the army came and went as if flying,was swift and fierce when attacking, and dexterous when retreating. King Wuling of Zhao made up his mind to learn from the non-Han nationalities, forming a powerful cavalry.

However, the ministers all rose against him. The Central Plains were a civilized place, and a state filled with ceremonies—these should have been followed by non-Han nationalities, who were not the teachers. After a great deal of struggle, King Wuling managed to persuade the opposition in his court. He then ordered the country to change into non-Han clothing. Then he converted the original border town of military importance—Yuanyang, where mainly soldiers and chariot troops were stationed—into a cavalry town. He ordered soldiers to take off their wide-sleeved robes, remove their heavy armors, put on non-Han short coats and long trousers, and undergo intense training in horse-riding and archery. Wuling personally trained this cavalry, and in less than a year, it was transformed. It can be said that "Wearing Non-Han Uniforms and Using Cavalry in Battles" is a well-known example in the trend of national integration.

The State of Qin in the northwest later emerged as a powerful nation in the Warring States Period. Qin was originally a branch of Quanrong, not a part of the Hua nationalities. Qin Xianggong was appointed as a vassal to King Dongping. Qin fought heavily with the Rong nationalities in the west, and finally dominated the West Rong at the turn of the Spring and Autumn Period and the Warring States Period, emerging as the center of merged nationalities in the west. Qin later became the most powerful state among seven kingdoms in the Warring States Period, after the Shang Yang political reform in 395 BC, Qin defeated the states of Han, Yue and Wei and merged the ethnic groups nearby. Moreover, Qin also

Meng Huo Being Caught Seven Times in Yinkeng, a New Year painting of the Qing Dynasty. It describes one of the wars of the Three Kingdoms, with which Zhuge Liang tried to conquer the southern people.

established counties of Qinzhong, Wu, Nan, Nanyang, Sanchuan and Taiyuan. The previously backward state under the Rong nationality finally emerged as the backbone and core of the Huaxia nationality.

The formation and development of ancient nationalities in China, from the Spring and Autumn Period to the Warring States Period, was magnificent and splendid. The Xia, Shang, Zhou, Chu, and Yue nationalities later played a dominant role in the great mergers of Chinese nationalities. In this historical drama, a new Huaxia nationality was established after the merger of various nationalities, featuring the State of Qi in the east, State of Qin in the west, states of Chu and Zhao in the south, and, State of Yan in the north. The establishment of the Huaxia nationality laid the base for the formation of a unified Han nationality, representing the second stage of the formation of the Han nationality.

3) The Han Nationality

The Huaxia nationality, originated from the great mergers of nationalities in the Spring and Autumn Period and the Warring States Period, was not a coherent and unified nation. At the time, the political situation required a unified center. To meet the needs of the time, Emperor Qin Shi Huang, a man of great talent and bold vision, unified China for the first time in 221 BC and established the first centralized feudal country—the Qin Dynasty (221-206 BC). The Huaxia nationality was thus united as one as well.

After the establishment of the Qin Dynasty, Qin Shi Huang adopted a system of prefectures and counties, stipulating that books had to be written in uniform characters. The emperor gave uniformity to currency, weights and measures, the distance between carriage wheels, and even social conduct. He also built the Great

Wall. All these measures helped unify and stabilize the Huaxia nationality.

Towards the end of the Qin Dynasty, Liu Bang and Xiang Yu revolted against the establishment. With his superior strength, Xiang Yu proclaimed himself the King of West Chu. Liu Bang was sent to Hanzhong, in present-day Shaanxi Province, and was appointed the King of Han. Subsequently, Liu Bang defeated XiangYu. Thus the dynasty set up by Liu Bang in 206 BC was called the Han Dynasty (206 BC-AD 220).

Unified measures adopted by Qin Shi Huang helped the Huaxia nationality become a stable community for people, and the Han Dynasty followed in his guiding footsteps. Han Emperor Wu established a provincial governor system, divided the nation into 13 prefectures, while politically implementing the household registration system. In economy, Han Emperor Wu introduced the *Junshu Act* and *Pingzhun Act* to control grain price. A nationwide commercial network, with the capital at its center, was established to facilitate the circulation of commodities. In terms of culture and ideology development, Han Emperor Wu developed Confucianism into classical studies. Confucianism gained prominence and became a critical part of the psychology of the emerging Han nationality. All these indicated that the "great unity" measures adopted by the central government of the Western Han Dynasty made the country more centralized and powerful. Unification had already been the mainstream of Chinese history, and the Huaxia nationality had also developed in the direction of finally forming the Han nationality.

The Han Dynasty, comprising the Western Han Dynasty (206 BC-AD 25) and Eastern Han Dynasty (25-220), lasted over 400 years, unlike the Qin Dynasty, which lasted only a short period of time. Much of this can be attributed to the fact that the Han

Dynasty boasted impressive military strength. In the Han Dynasty, other nationalities called the soldiers of the Han "Han soldiers", envoys of the Han "Han envoys", and people of the Han "Han people". Han became the name of the Huaxia nationality, and the Han nationality.

The Han nationality, with its huge population, went on to become one of the most prominent nations in the world. After its formation, the Han nationality, with its unparalleled stability, power and ambition, embarked on a quest to establish itself as one of the great nations of the world. A snowball effect made the Hans extremely powerful and influential, and the effect continues till today.

China has been a multi-national country since ancient times. Now China is home to 56 nationalities. The splendid history and culture of China have been created by various nationalities.

In Chinese history, two dynasties were built by minority nationalities. The Yuan Dynasty (1279-1368) for instance, was established by a Mongolian minority group. A unified and recon-structed multi-national country with a vast territory was estab-lished. Despite a few temporary separations, China maintained its unification process for 700 years, from the Yuan Dynasty till present day. This long-term unification facilitated the development of and interaction among various nationalities.

The second was the Qing Dynasty (1644-1911) established by Jurchens (i.e. the Manchu nationality) in the northeast. After the Qing Dynasty chose Beijing as its capital in 1644, a large number of people of the Manchu nationality entered the Shanhai Pass, while people from the Han nationality migrated to northeastern China. The two nationalities then co-existed peacefully. The unifi-cation of a multi-national country was consolidated and further developed after the establishment of the Qing Dynasty. Monan-

Mongolia, Mobei Khalkha Mongolia and Moxi Elute Mongolia in the north and northwest were unified. In the Western Regions Yili General was posted, and a provincial system was established in Xinjiang in 1884. Measures were also adopted to maintain and consolidate the unification of Tibet. The Taiwan Prefecture was established under Fujian Province. Taiwan became a province in 1885. The territory of the People's Republic of China was defined by the Qing Dynasty, and its various nationalities live in a unified China.

Several millennia have shown that the establishment of China and unification of the country were achieved by various nationalities. They safeguarded China's vast territory in the northeast, north, northwest and south. This period of national unification and friendly interaction between various nationalities comprised two thirds of the entire history of China. With consolidated unification and reduced separation, a profound and long-term friendship between various nationalities was developed.

2. Formation and Development of the Chinese Nation

The Chinese nation is a generic term for various nationalities in China, and it implies that the basic and long-term interests of various nationalities shall never be separated.

The Chinese nation originated and developed in a historical period beginning with the Xia Dynasty, before Qin unified China. It sprang up from the middle and lower reaches of the Yellow River. The Huaxia nationality had basically taken shape in the Xia, Shang, and Zhou dynasties. It was formed after a national merger, during the Spring and Autumn Period and the Warring States Period. In addition, the Diqiang and Dongyi nationalities were formed at that time. Many nationalities along the border areas originated and evolved accordingly, establishing increasingly closer relations with the Central Plains.

A great unifying period occurred during the Qin and Han dynasties (221BC-AD 220). The Huaxia nationality evolved into the Han nationality against a backdrop of grand unification. The Huaxia nationality also united with various other nationalities at that time, laying a territorial foundation for a unified multi-national country. The south and north of China were governed by the Han nationality and the minority nationalities respectively, from 220 to 581, before the establishment of the Sui Dynasty (581-618). During that time, separatist regimes were set up by different forces. Then both areas became unified within their own respective territories, causing constant and long-term confrontation between the Southern and Northern Dynasties (420-581). Minority nationalities in the north had already been part of China's ethnic groups, and had gained a clear picture of China's politics and culture as they moved forward to fight for role as the "legitimate ruler of China" with dynasties established by the Hans. Previously, only the Han people could be called Chinese, and now "China" was to be a common title for various nationalities.

The Central Plains were unified during the Sui and Tang (618-907) dynasties, after the separatist regimes in the Southern and Northern Dynasties. A unified multi-national country was being formed. China's territory had been consolidated based on the Qin and Han dynasties. Moreover, the Sui and Tang dynasties featured one important development for the Chinese nation. Specifically, after the unification of Tibet, the Tubo Dynasty rose and established sound relations with the Tang Dynasty, helping to integrate Tibet with China.

The Liao (916-1125) and Jin (1115-1234) dynasties established prefectures and counties in all of northeastern China, and introduced a clan and tribe military commissioner system in pastoral areas. As a result, the local administrative system in the two places was improved, greatly helping to consolidate the Chinese territory. Other regional dynasties or border dynasties in places like the Bohai Sea, Nanzhao, Xixia, Dali and Xiliao all followed the political systems adopted in the Sui and Tang dynasties, and were greatly influenced by the Han culture despite their different locations and characteristics.

China adopted an open foreign policy during the Sui and Tang dynasties, Liao Dynasty, Jin Dynasty, Northern Song Dynasty (960-1127) and Southern Song Dynasty (1127-1279). Its economy and culture boomed magically during the time. China also established closer relations with the rest of the world.

The Yuan (1279-1368), Ming (1368-1644) and Qing (1644-1911) dynasties entered a period characterized by a unified multi-national country. Nationalities across the country were under the control of the central government. The boundaries between China and its neighboring countries had been identified. Various nationalities in China were already familiar with the concept of country, demonstrating that the overall national consciousness of the Chinese nation had emerged.

During the period from 1840 to that before the 1911 Revolution, the Chinese nation strived to protect its sovereignty and territorial integrity, and established a republic after overthrowing the 2,000-year-old monarchy system. Compared with ancient times, the Chinese nation featured increased patriotism in its effort to fight against imperialism and feudalism.

The Chinese nationality was unified politically during the period lasting from the end of the 1911 Revolution to the time before the establishment of the People's Republic of China in 1949. Imperialism, feudalism and bureaucratic capitalism were finally overthrown, and China was liberated. Since the establishment of the new China, the country has entered a period featuring revitalization and booming development.

Chapter 5

Rise and Fall of the Dynasties

China's history witnessed frequent dynastic changes. The decline of an empire was often accompanied by a major peasant uprising. After the war ended, a new empire would rise from the ruins of the former dynasty. The death of the Qin Dynasty (221-206 BC) and the prosperity of the Han Dynasty (206 BC-AD 220) would come to represent the most profound renewal, in the memories of future generations. Where there was decline, there was prosperity. The Golden Years of Zhenguan (627-649), the Peace and Prosperity of the Kaiyuan Years (713-741) during the great Tang Dynasty (618-907), and the Flourishing Years of Kangxi (1662-1723) and Qianlong (1736-1796) during the Qing Dynasty (1644-1911) are prime examples of the country's prosperity during its feudal era.

1. Fall of the Qin Dynasty and Rise of the Han Dynasty

Several anti-Qin military forces emerged along with the peasant uprising led by Chen Sheng and Wu Guang, in the late Qin Dynasty. Among them, Xiang Yu and Liu Bang were the two main forces. They gained support from the ordinary people during the anti-Qin wars and their power grew quickly. Attacked by the main forces of Liu Bang and Xiang Yu, the Qin Dynasty came to an abrupt end in 206 BC.

Liu Bang wanted to live in the imperial palace after occupying Xianyang. Fan Kuai and Zhang Liang persuaded him not to get too greedy for the treasures and pleasures the throne offered. Liu Bang accepted what they suggested and sent troops to Bashang. He also abolished a few severe laws of the Qin Dynasty, and established a new law, which stated that murderers would be killed, and attackers and thieves severely punished. Liu was greatly supported and favored by the ordinary people due to what he had done.

But elsewhere, Xiang Yu was offended when he heard that Liu Bang had entered Central Shaanxi first. Xiang Yu led his troops, seizing Hangu Pass and then sweeping into Xianyang. Four hundred thousand soldiers were deployed in Xinfeng (now northeast of Lintong County, Shaanxi) and Hongmen (now Xiang-wangying, east of Lintong County) in December, 206 BC. Liu Bang's troops were outnumbered and doomed; he had a mere 100,000 soldiers at the time. Following Zhang Liang's suggestion, Liu Bang visited Xiang Yu in Hongmeng. Liu first apologized to Xiang Yu with modest and humble words. Xiang Yu then hosted a banquet in Liu Bang's honor. Xiang Yu's advisor Fan Zeng planned to kill Liu Bang, and asked a brave soldier, Xiang Zhuang, Xiang Yu's younger brother, to assassinate him while performing a sword dance. Xiang Yu's uncle Xiang Bo, who had a sound personal rapport with Zhang Liang, discovered the conspiracy. Presently, Liu Bang excused himself on the pretext of going to the bathroom, and escaped to Bashang.

Subsequently, Xiang Yu took his troops to Xianyang, killed Ying, prince of the Qin Dynasty, burnt down Qin's palace and declared himself King of Western Chu. He also appointed Liu Bang as King of Han and awarded him Sichuan and Central Shaanxi. Xiang Yu offered his officials land around Pengcheng to consolidate the alliance; but some of the others were dissatisfied and complained, since they couldn't get the land of their choice. Conflicts were becoming increasingly evident. Wars between vassal states broke out again.

Liu Bang, who had been compelled to relocate to the small, remote places of Sichuan and Central Shaanxi, followed Xiao He's strategy of hiring talented people in Central Shaanxi, and made Sichuan his base. Liu Bang conquered Central Shaanxi in May, 206 BC, while Xiang Yu led his troops to fight against Tian Rong. Then Liu Bang took his troops eastward and attacked Xiang Yu's base, Pengcheng. The Chu-Han War took place from 206 BC to 202 BC between Xiang Yu and Liu Bang, with almost 70 large-scale battles and 40 small ones over five years. Liu Bang repeatedly failed, but was not discouraged. Finally, Liu Bang dispatched Han Xin to the north to occupy places such as states of Zhao, Wei and Qi, and the second battleground was established. Liu Bang also united with other dukes and wooed Peng Yue and Ying Bu to isolate Xiang Yu, turning the tide against his enemy gradually.

Left without any allies, Xiang Yu was compelled to divide the country into two, with a boundary called Honggou (present-day Jialu River, Henan Province). The western part of Honggou was assigned to Liu Bang (Han) and the east to himself (Chu).

Following his ministers' suggestion, Liu Bang gathered his dukes to surround Xiang Yu in Gaixia (southeast of present-day Lingbi County, Anhui Province), towards the end of 203 BC. Xiang Yu did not have access to supplies or reinforcements, and was under siege at the top of a mountain on a cold winter night. When he saw banners everywhere and heard the horns and drums, Xiang Yu realized that defeat was inevitable. He had no choice but to bid farewell to his beloved concubine Yu Ji, and escape at night.

Liu Bang sent 5,000 soldiers after Xiang Yu at dawn. Xiang Yu's troops crossed the Huaihe River, with only 100 soldiers surviving. They were followed by the Han army and killed. Xiang Yu then ran to the side of the Wujiang River. He threw himself on his sword, facing the vast water ahead and with his enemies pressing upon him from behind.

Farewell, My Concubine, painted by Zhang Huibin

Liu Bang went on to unite China, established the Han Dynasty in June 206 BC and proclaimed himself emperor (Gaozu of the Han Dynasty).

The Chu-Han War evolved directly from peasant uprisings at the end of the Qin Dynasty, but with a different nature. Though the old feudal dynasty was overthrown by the peasant uprising, Liu Bang and Xiang Yu, former leaders of the peasant insurgency, followed the beaten path of feudal ruling. They were interested only in getting the throne eventually. Xiang Yu, typical of old aristocrats, was incapable of using his skills as a ruler or building a unified dynasty. Liu Bang, in sharp contrast, was good at picking the right people and adopting effective strategies at the right time.

He finally defeated Xiang Yu and set up the Western Han Dynasty (206 BC-AD 25).

The Chinese introduced the battle formations of the Chu-Han War into Chinese chess. It was said that "Chu He Han Jie" (Chu River and Han Boundary) on the chessboard evolved from this famous war. This is the origin of present-day Chinese chess. Passed down and studied generation after generation, various kinds of chess manuals are available now. Even today, the Chinese are interested in studying new Chinese chess strategies, with all the wonder and fun accompanying them.

2. The Splendid Tang Dynasty

The Tang Dynasty (618-907) represents a golden period in China's ancient history, and featured national strength, transparent politics, booming economy, peace and culture. The Tang Dynasty boasts impressive achievements on the cultural, political, economic, and diplomatic fronts. It was one of the superpowers worldwide. Its neighboring East Asian countries, including Xinluo, Bohai and Japan, were greatly influenced, politically and culturally. The national strength of the Tang Dynasty overshadowed that of other dynasties in Chinese history.

During its prime, the Tang Dynasty stretched to the Korean Peninsula in the east, Central Asia in the west, Vietnam in the south and Baikal Lake in the north. The Dynasty established six prefectures including Anxi, Anbei, Andong, Annan, Chanyu, and Beiting, for the sound management of Tujue (Turk), Huihe (Uygur), Mohe, Tiele, Shiwei and Qidan (Khitan), among others.

The Mongolian Plateau, controlled by Tujue, was a part of Tang's sphere of influence, under the governance of Li Shimin or Emperor Taizong, the second emperor of the Tang Dynasty. The ethnic groups in the north even called the emperor the Heavenly Khan. With regard to internal affairs, the prime ministerial system was followed; the Three Departments and Six Ministries system, and Imperial Examination, were also adopted and improved. Moreover, the Equal-Field system and Tax-Labor-Substitution system were introduced during the time. Emperor Taizong brought together a large number of talents, regardless of their family background. This period, defined by stable social order and a booming economy, has been called the Golden Years of Zhenguan (627-649). Its main political achievements were enshrined in text books for emperors in Japan and North Korea, followed by emperors of later generations.

Li Shimin (Emperor Taizong, founder of the Tang Dynasty), painted by Yan Liben of the Tang Dynasty

During the 44-year reign of Emperor Xuanzong, the Tang Dynasty reached its peak, a golden age, a period of governance and sound economic development. The period has been called the Great Reign of the Kaiyuan Years (713-741), and regarded as the second most prosperous time in Chinese history after Emperor Wu's reign of the Han Dynasty. Its capital Chang'an was also the biggest metropolis in the world at the time.

Emperor Taizong did everything in his power to make the country prosperous, during the beginning of the peaceful Zhenguan period. He knew that only skill could lead to peaceful and efficient governance, and that talents should be evaluated by morality and knowledge. The emperor also made great efforts to develop culture and education. A complete official educational system under the central and local governments was established. Imperial schools, and the study of temperament and arithmetics were set up; schools were also established in prefectures and counties. The establishment of imperial school, the highest level of state academy, was followed closely by Emperor Taizong.

The emperor also issued an order to set up a Confucius Temple for the imperial school; Confucius was hailed as a sage while Yan Hui became known as a great teacher in the second year of Zhenguan (628). An opening ceremony commemorating Confucius was held every year at a fixed time; the size of the schools was expanded, with an additional 1,200 rooms. Confucian scholars were treated extremely well, with the government paying their traveling expenses and bringing them to the capital in carriages. Any student who mastered one classical book (the imperial annotations of *Laozi*, *Filial Piety*, to be mastered within three years) was offered an official post. Emperor Taizong also personally inspected imperial schools, assigning renowned Confucian scholars to the schools. Directors and principal teachers were required to offer lessons on the spot, and were often awarded.

Rulers stipulated that poetry-composing skills would be tested in the imperial examination, which greatly promoted the development of culture. The Tang Dynasty was a golden age for literature, poetry, essays and legendary novels. In particular, poems of diversified styles and different schools were crowned the gems of Tang-Dynasty literature. Many renowned poets emerged in that period, their magnificent poems a precious wealth left to later generations. After Chen Zi'ang and the four distinguished poets in early Tang, renowned poets emerged in an endless stream. Li Bai, Du Fu, Cen Sen, and Wang Wei in prime Tang, Li He, Han Yu, and Bai Juyi in middle Tang and Li Shangyin, Du Mu in late Tang. Their poems featured rich mythical imagery, detailed descriptions of real life, historical poems, as well as fresh and refined pastoral poems. Though outstanding poets appeared in the Song, Ming and Qing dynasties, their skills in *Lushi* (a classical poem of eight lines, each containing five or seven characters, with a strict tonal pattern and rhyme scheme) and ancient poetry never surpassed the talents of the poets in the Tang Dynasty.

Short stories developed on the basis of the tradition of the literary sketches in the Six Dynasties (222-589), namely, the Kingdom of Wu (222-280), the Eastern Jin Dynasty (317-420), the Song Dynasty (420-479), the Qi Dynasty (479-502), the Liang Dynasty (502-557) and the Chen Dynasty (557-589). The novel of the Tang Dynasty was marked by an integrated story structure and complete connections among the characters, mirroring society. Masterpieces of short stories in the Tang Dynasty included *Pillow Note*, *The Story of Ying-Ying* and *The Story of Li Wa*, among others. All these works laid a solid foundation for the rapid development of story-tellers' scripts in the Song Dynasty (960-1279), and the novels of the Ming (1368-1644) and Qing (1644-1911) dynasties.

A tolerant religious policy was adopted in the early Tang Dynasty. Two traditional religions—Buddhism and Taoism— developed rapidly. Forty percent of the mural paintings and sculptures in the Mogao Grottoes of Dunhuang, for instance, were based on the works of the Tang Dynasty. Eminent monk Xuan Zang went to Tianzhu (present-day India) to gather 657 Buddhist Sutras for the Tang Dynasty, and the government subsequently built the Dayan (Big Wild Goose) Pagoda to keep these scripts safe. The massive translations of Buddhist classics and the increase in the number of monks in China fuelled the unprecedented development of Buddhism in the country. The main factions of Buddhism had taken shape. Other religions, including Islam, Nestorianism, and Mazdaism, all spread to China due to international

Monk Xuan Zang

慈恩唐三藏玄奘法師

influence.

During the Tang Dynasty outstanding achievements were also made in the field of natural sciences. For example, an astronomer monk named Yixing measured the length of the meridians. The "Medicine God" Sun Simiao wrote an unusual book on medicine, *Thousand Golden Prescriptions*. The printing of the *Vajracchedika Sutra* in 868 is acknowledged as the earliest block printing in the world. And the technologies of paper- and textile-making spread to as far as West Asia and Europe, through Arabia.

The Tang Dynasty adopted an open foreign policy and established diplomatic ties with over 70 countries worldwide. The government also implemented an enlightened policy in governing the country and a policy of mollification in places where ethnic groups, who had submitted to the Tang Dynasty, lived. Eight hundred and fifty-six Jimi prefectures and counties with a high degree of autonomy were set up. Emperor Taizong viewed people from all ethnic groups equally, and once said, "China has always been cherished, while ethnic groups like Yi and Di have been despised since ancient times; yet I love them and treat them equally."

Princess Wencheng was sent by the emperor to Tubo to marry Songtsan Gambo, King of Tubo, in 641. Then Princess Jincheng was sent to marry Mes-ag-tshoms, to forge an alliance and bring the advanced culture of the Tang Dynasty to Tubo. Tubo and the Tang Dynasty forged an alliance, defined their territory and declared mutual nonaggression in 822. The Tang-Tubo Alliance Monument has been preserved in Jokhang Monastery, Lhasa. The Tang Dynasty

Tang Dynasty Ffficials Meeting Envoys from the Byzantine Empire, a mural painting in the tomb of Prince Li Xian of the Tang Dynasty, Qian County, Shaanxi Province

and Nanzhao (local regime in Yunnan Province in the 8-10th centuries) formed an alliance in Diancang Mountain in 794, establishing sound mutual relations. The Tang Dynasty boasted solid unity with ethnic groups including Tubo and Tuguhun, thanks to these measures. The government also appointed leaders of the ethnic groups as officials, and assigned them to lead troops as a way of showing great trust in them. All his successors followed what Emperor Taizong did, promoting the interaction between China and foreign countries, and facilitating the merger between the Han and other nationalities.

Princess Wencheng Entering Tibet, butter sculpture made on the 15th day of the New Year at Ta'er Monastery, Huangzhong County, Qinghai Province

Emperor Taizong attached great importance to the development of education. The measures enforced by Emperor Taizong were then followed by Emperor Gaozong, Empress Wu Zetian (Tse-tien) and Emperor Xuanzong. They continually improved school education, created a talent pool for the dynasty, thereby securing the prosperity of the Tang Dynasty. The well-developed education system also brought many benefits to its neighboring counties, helping to facilitate the development there. Japan and Xinluo sent a large number of scholars to study in the Tang Dynasty. These scholars brought back home advanced systems, including the equal-land system, legal system and imperial examination system, and social reforms achieved great success. They combined their native language with Chinese and created a new written language. They learned medicine and astronomy, and then spread the knowledge in their own country.

Against this backdrop, Buddhism was brought to Japan and Xinluo, exerting a profound influence on the societies there. Some overseas students even lived in China for a long time, reading Chinese classics, applying for official positions and writing books. Abe Nakamaro or Chao Heng, from Japan, was good at composing poetry and essays. He had a close personal relation with poets Li Bai and Wang Wei. They often drank and sang together while composing poems. Abe was appointed the deputy chief censor and secretary supervisor, and died at 73 in China. Noblemen of Tubo came from the remote snow-coated plateau to learn the decrees, regulations, ceremonies and customs of the Tang Dynasty, as well as the classics of Confucianism and Buddhism.

The ties between Tubo and the Tang Dynasty had been greatly cemented. Tubo occupied the Gansu area after the armed rebellion led by An Lushan and Shi Siming in 755. According to materials in the Mogao Grottoes of Dunhuang, Tubo still adhered to some regulations, ceremonies and customs of the Tang Dynasty, and respected Buddhism and Confucian scholars. For instance, the government sent people to copy Buddhist scriptures and *Filial Piety*. "Shidian", the opening ceremony designated to commemorate Confucius, was held at a fixed time in schools every year.

All these helped the Tang Dynasty to strengthen cultural and personal interactions with its neighboring countries and become a dominating global player.

Merchants, diplomats, monks and overseas students from many countries flocked to China in prime Tang. Large numbers of foreigners and ethnic groups lived along the Silk Road, and in places such as Chang'an, Luoyang, Guangzhou, and Yangzhou. Chang'an was an international metropolis at the time. Honglu Temple, for example, an organization set up to accommodate diplomats and guests, was home to over 4,000 foreigners. Many merchants from Central Asia and West Asia peddled in the West Market of Chang'an. Beautiful women from foreign countries were hired by pubs to attract more customers.

Tricolor porcelain camel with musicians, Tang Dynasty

The poet Li Bai often went to the pub and chanted, "Beauties from abroad look like flowers and sell wines with great smiles like the spring breeze."

In addition, many neighboring ethnic groups migrated to Chang'an. Tens of thousands of families from Tujue (Turkey), for instance, moved to Chang'an. A large number of foreigners settled down in the Tang Dynasty, living together with the Han people. They married and had kids there, or changed their citizenship to Tang. They also brought their own cultures, customs, food, clothing, entertainment, and even religious beliefs, exerting a profound impact on the Tang Dynasty.

Persian and Arabic merchants also came to the Tang Dynasty by land and sea. They were well known for selling jewelry, and making huge profits. Certain foods, including spinach, candied dates, and skills such as sword-swallowing and fire-eating, spread to the Tang Dynasty, while handicraft technologies such as paper-making and brocade-making were passed onto the West.

Islamism, Mazdaism, Nestorianism and Manicheanism were brought to the inner land of the Tang Dynasty with the arrival of people from the Western Regions. All of these foreign religions, the widespread Indian Buddhism in particular, penetrated all aspects of the Tang Dynasty, having a great impact on its philosophy, literature, linguistics, architecture, art, etc.

A large number of foreigners and ethnic groups nearby flocked to Chang'an during the Kaiyuan and Tianbao periods. They lived together with the Han people for a long time. The Hu people even ascended to prominent positions in the Tang Dynasty, causing great concern to the ordinary people. Instead of curbing the trend, the Tang Dynasty was active in absorbing the cream of foreign cultures in order to enrich itself; it integrated the customs and people into the Chinese civilization as a way to create a more colorful culture. It showed its own powerful vision, adhering to the saying, "The great ocean is able to accommodate hundreds of rivers while the great mind is able to accommodate thousands of different views."

3. The Heyday of the Kangxi and Qianlong Periods

The Flourishing Years of the Kangxi and Qianlong refers to a stable and prosperous period in the early period of the Qing Dynasty. It lasted from Emperor Kangxi's reign to the middle of Emperor Qianlong's reign, representing the final booming period for China's feudal dynasties. Specifically, this period lasted over

130 years, from 1662 to 1795, with Kangxi, Yongzheng and Qianlong as the three emperors. The rulers adopted and implemented political and economic measures that would ease class imbalances and friction among nationalities so as to safeguard a unified multi-national country and secure long-term stability in a society where people lived and worked contentedly. The country was just stepping out of the trauma left over by wars in the late Ming Dynasty and early Qing Dynasty. The economy enjoyed rapid development and the Qing Dynasty also emerged as one of the most powerful nations in the world.

Emperor Kangxi (1654-1722) led the dynasty to its peak time. He was called Aixinjueluo Xuanye, the second emperor after the Qing Dynasty entered the Shanhai Pass. Kangxi succeeded the imperial throne at the age of eight, in 1661. Suggested by the empress dowager, his father, Emperor Shunzhi, appointed four ministers, Suoni, Ebilong, Sukesaha and Aobai, to help him administrate the country. Later the state powers fell into the hands of Aobai, a go-getting and arrogant person, who also established a clique secretly for himself. After killing Aobai at the age of 16, Emperor Kangxi began to exercise monarchial power. Kangxi made impressive achievements in both civilized governance and military control.

First, Kangxi consolidated and strengthened the country's unification, making the greatest contributions to Chinese history. He firmly quelled rebellions launched by three local authorities, tightened control over southern China while unifying Taiwan. Kangxi dispatched troops to expel Russian invaders deployed in Jaxa, Heilongjiang basin, in 1675, containing their ambition to attack China. He sent representatives to sign the Treaty of Nerchinsk in 1679, defining the boundary between eastern China and Russia. The emperor also quelled the rebellions in Huijiang and Zhunggar launched by aristocrats. Revolts in Greater Jinchuan and Lesser Jinchuan (today's northwest part of Sichuan Province), armed riots led by Dahezhuomu and Xiaohezhuomu in Xinjiang, and Gurkha's attack against Tibet were all suppressed during Qianlong's reign. The unified multi-national country were consolidated, and aggression from the western powers was contained.

China's vast territory stretched from Stanovoy Range (Outer Hinggan Range) in the north, Nansha Islands in the south, to Balkhash Lake and Pamirs in the west, and Sea of Okhotsk, Sakhal Island and Taiwan in the east, from Kangxi's regime to the middle of the 19th century. With cemented national unification and strengthened centralized power, China had become a unified country with vast territory and strong national strengths, laying a solid foundation for its socioeconomic development. It is safe to say that Emperor Kangxi did a great job in governing the Qing Dynasty, while laying the foundation for the Flourishing Years of Kangxi and Qianlong.

Prosperity of the Kangxi and Qianlong years was obvious in agriculture, handicraft industry, commerce and so on.

Kangxi issued an order in 1669 to stop the enclosure policy introduced in the early Qing Dynasty, declaring that civilians and soldiers from the Manchu and Han nationalities would be treated equally. Farmers got back their lands, and were allowed to explore and cultivate wild lands. As a way to ease tension between employees and employers, wealthy and powerful families could not bully tenants. Land tax was reduced or removed, and miscellaneous levies were all relieved. The emperor announced that the amount of silver per person in 1711 would be taken as a benchmark, and the government would never levy additional taxes. Measures pertaining to "the combination of land and labor tax" and "labor allocated per *mu*" were adopted during Yongzheng's period, an improvement on the "single whip" system introduced in the Ming Dynasty. All of these measures alleviated farmers' burden and eased class imbalance. The feudal order was gradually stabilized and agricultural production enjoyed recovery and

Farming in the Qing Dynasty

development, evidenced by the expanded arable land. According to statistics, the arable land nationwide reached over 6.07 million hectares in the 24th year of Kangxi's reign (1685), and 8.9 million hectares under Yongzheng's reign. Actually, these were incomplete statistics, since landlords concealed the amount of land they had, and some ethnic groups were unable to count.

The population size also increased sharply along with land. The population during the Ming Dynasty was registered at over 60 million, 19 million under Shunzhi's regime and 60 million in Kangxi's reign. The figure even surged to 140 million during the Qianlong years.

Impressive achievements were scored in water conservation during the early Qing Dynasty. Projects included flood control of the Yellow River and dredging of the Yongding River. Productivity was greatly improved. The Qing Dynasty boasted a high grain output. Grains increasingly became a part of commodity circulation, and agriculture developed rapidly, laying a solid foundation for the prosperity of the Qing Dynasty.

The handicraft industry flourished. The tax reforms of the Qing Dynasty further loosened the handicraftsmen and merchants' reliance on the feudal dynasty. Their social status was greatly improved. Rulers in the Qing Dynasty also eased restrictions on the handicraft industry, promoting the development of commerce and industry. Family handicraft industries in places like areas south of the Yangtze River, Sichuan Province, and Hubei Province, well known for their reel weaving, developed faster even as various kinds of manual workshops mushroomed. The silk-weaving industry in Suzhou and Hangzhou, the porcelain industry in Jingdezhen, and the salt-boiling industry in Sichuan witnessed sound development, as did the sugar industry, tea industry and tobacco industry. Massive copper mining happened in Yunnan Province during the reigns of Yongzheng and Qianlong. The development of the handicraft industry far surpassed that of the Ming Dynasty, with greatly increased production efficiency, and bigger output and variety.

Bumper supply facilitated the prosperity of commerce nationwide, and many commercial cities and trade ports emerged. Beijing was the national trade center and chinaware, earthenware, silk fabrics, cloth, copper, liquor, etc. were all important goods at the time. Foreign trade also flourished. The first seeds of capitalism emerged in some well-developed cities. The Flourishing Years of the Kangxi and Qianlong was the last period of prosperity for the feudal dynasties of China.

Chapter 6

Diversified Religions

China is a multi-religion country, differing from the practices among many medieval countries or regions that unify politics and religion, or believe in a single religion and exclude infidels. The country not only embraces local born religions, but some foreign religions as well. Generally, these religions co-exist peacefully with one another, and they even blend with and absorb each other.

China's most influential religions are Buddhism, Taoism, and Islam; Christianity also began to spread to China in the early Tang Dynasty (618-907), but its introduction went on and off, and it did not take root in China until the 19th century. In addition, although strictly speaking the Confucian doctrine is not a religion, it was part of the mainstream of Chinese culture and had a profound impact on the people, with respect to their thinking and behavior patterns. It thus possessed a status similar to the other religions.

1. How Confucianism Was Enshrined As a Religion

Confucius and his Confucian school are now universally known. However, at the beginning of the school's creation in the Spring and Autumn Period (770-476 BC) and Warring States Period (475-221 BC), it was only one of many and held no particularly lofty status. At the time, Confucius with his students was peddling his political views everywhere, while the national leaders were busy fighting for influence and expansion of their own forces. Not one of them showed any respect to him.

After Qin Shi Huang unified the country, he ruled his people with a severely disciplinary hand, and this was one of the contributors to the rapid decline and fall of the Qin Dynasty (221-206 BC). In the early period of the Western Han Dynasty (206 BC-AD 25), the Han rulers learned lessons from the quick death of the Qin Dynasty. They took Huangdi's and Laozi's (see next section) "noninterference approach" to let the people recuperate and multiply, to reduce their burdens so they could develop production actively. Soon enough a strong and prosperous situation emerged.

During Emperor Wu's reign (141-87 BC) of the Han Dynasty, a new series of problems started to become apparent: the princes became stronger in force, showing a tendency of incompliance; property owners began to increasingly exploit farmers, the conflicts between them heating up. Emperor Wu was a man of great political talent and aspiration. He tended to implement positive policies to strengthen the centralization of power, and his national power enabled him to do so. To this end, since the guiding theory governing the country needed to be updated, a new force, Confucianism, whose propositions were both positive and fashionable, suddenly rose, and achieved political and ideological dominance.

In 134 BC, Emperor Wu summoned famous scholars from all over the country to the capital, personally soliciting their opinions about administering the country.

Dong Zhongshu (179-104 BC) pointed out in his counter-measures: Now different theories coexisted and their purposes were not the same, so the country did not have unified governance philosophy, which put the officials in a quandary. Therefore, he suggested to prohibit the dissemination and development of all other theories, except the Confucian doctrine. The core of Dong Zhongshu's proposal was to achieve unity of thinking, a concept of complete unification that was very much in line with Emperor Wu's political need for the establishment of a unified empire. The proposal therefore received full recognition from Emperor Wu. The establishment of the overwhelming position of Confucianism helped the concept of complete unification strike root in the hearts of people in China, and became one of the important traditions of Chinese culture.

Dong Zhongshu

Of course, Dong Zhongshu's Confucianism was different in meaning from the original Confucian doctrine. It was a new doctrine that absorbed and combined various other theories and ideas. It was under the guidance of the idea of complete unification and the new Confucian doctrine that Emperor Wu took a series of measures to strengthen the centralization of power, and wherever possible, to centralize all power into his own hands. He strengthened his power over the socio-economy, unified currency, established a government monopoly on salt, iron, and wine, and unified tax standards, which amassed him a huge wealth that would provide for his political and military pursuits. He carved out new territories, attacking the Huns in the north, suppressing the Baiyue people's riot in the south, and forcing his way into the Western Regions. Through these initiatives, he established an unprecedentedly unified and powerful empire. Nearly all the later emperors of great talent and bold vision in various dynasties adopted similar ruling measures.

The Confucianism established by Dong Zhongshu met the needs of successive rulers of various dynasties, therefore they inherited it. With the introduction of Buddhism and the rise of Taoism, by the Sui (581-618) and Tang (618-907) dynasties, the version of the three religions—Confucianism, Buddhism and Taoism—was already a very popular view. Buddhism and Taoism had both suffered exclusion and suppression that were comparatively more serious, but the status of Confucianism was relatively stable. By the Song Dynasty (960-1279), Confucianism had entered another stage of development, forming a complete system of philosophy, the core of which was Ideals. Thus it was called Idealism, and Western scholars generally called it Neo-Confucianism.

After the establishment of the imperial examination system, proficiency in the Confucian classics became the most important condition needed for an official career. In the Ming (1368-1644) and Qing (1644-1911) dynasties, especially, annotated versions of the "Four Books" by Zhu Xi (1130-1200) had become the basis for the imperial examination. Confucianism became the only content of school education; the candidate could only state views in the name of the "saint", without being given the freedom to play with his own ideas. Confucianism was sanctified, and it attained the status similar to that of a religion. The code of ethics and standards of conduct set by it became deeply rooted in the hearts of the

Chinese people, turning into a fundamental law that China's people consciously esteemed.

Clearly, Confucianism is only a theory, not a religion, but in the eyes of foreigners, the Chinese people's attitude towards it had no much difference from regarding it as a religion, and they also gave it some form of religion. The first major manifestation is the blind embrace of Confucianism, and the second is the deification of Confucius.

In his time, Confucius was already known as a saint. Successive rulers granted him a series of honorable names, far superior to those of general emperors and having a divine implication. He became respected and worshiped by rulers and scholars of various dynasties. The hometown of Confucius in Qufu, Shandong Province became the Holy Land that included the Confucian Residence, the Confucian Temple, Confucian Woods (including

The Dacheng Hall of Beijing's Confucian Temple, in front of which is a board inscribed with the words "An Exemplary Teacher for All Ages" in the calligraphy of Qing Emperor Kangxi.

Confucian Tomb), all of which were sacred and inviolable. Emperor Qianlong of the Qing Dynasty (1644-1911) personally worshipped Confucius in Qufu eight times.

Confucius' direct descendants were awarded various titles, following the Han Dynasty. In the Song Dynasty they were granted the title "Father of Saint", which was passed down through successive dynasties until the Qing Dynasty perished. After the founding of the Republic of China, the title was changed into "Sacrificial Official for the Great Sage", hereditary ever since. Confucian Temples were built all over China, housing the memorial tablets of Confucius and his major disciples. Each year government officials would hold memorial services there. The most famous Confucian Temple is in Beijing, covering 20,000 square meters, and at the main hall is suspended a board, with the legend, "An Exemplary Teacher for All Ages", handwritten by Emperor Kangxi of the Qing Dynasty. Other schools had also established memorial tablets of "The Great Sage and Teacher Confucius", and before going to school, the students would first salute before the tablet, and hold a worshiping ceremony for Confucius.

In short, since the Han Dynasty, Confucian doctrines became an official ideology, with strong religious overtones. They became revered beliefs in various Chinese dynasties and an important component of the country's cultural psychology.

2. Kung Fu and Taoism

It can be said that kung fu is one of China's business cards. One can still see the elderly practicing *taiji* in China's urban parks. Due to historical reasons, people today tend to associate kung fu with Taoism.

Taoism is a native Chinese religion. Because it regards "Tao" as the supreme belief, the governor of the universe, the intrinsic thing that turns into everything in the universe; it is all-encompassing and ubiquitous, so it is called "Taoism". Its core belief is the pursuit of longevity and immortality through taking pills of immortality and cultivating vital energy.

Taoist origins are complex, spanning the pre-Qin period's faith in supernatural beings, the doctrine of *Qi* (vital energy), primitive sorcery, and Huangdi's and Laozi's ideas. The longevity

and immortality of supernatural beings are the goals pursued by Taoism. *Qi* is something that makes people become immortal, turning them into gods of longevity. Witchcraft is the basis of Taoist practicing methods. Huangdi and Laozi represent peace and quiet and noninterference. Huangdi's ideological course is based on legend, whereas Laozi (with the name Li Dan or Li Er) is the founder of Taoism, which regards Huangdi's and Laozi's thinking as its ideological foundation, esteeming them as its founders.

Since Emperor Wu respected only Confucianism, part of the Huang-Lao

Taoist Alchemist, a painting by Huang Shen of the Qing Dynasty

school converted to faith in supernatural beings after losing power and influence; they began to pursue supernatural methods of health preservation, and in the late Eastern Han Dynasty (25-220), formed the Tao of Peace and the Tao of Five-*Dou* (a unit of dry measure of grain)-of-Rice. The Tao of Peace was preached through such methods as letting people drink incanted water, or curing people of their diseases through incantation. They had hundreds of thousands of followers. The Tao of Five-*Dou*-of-Rice asked their followers to stress integrity, to treat diseases using retreats, to correct mental and behavioral mistakes, and to dispense rice and meat by the roadside for passers-by to eat freely. The establishment of the Tao of Peace and the Tao of Five-*Dou*-of-Rice marked the formation of Taoism.

The main body of initial Taoist believers was the underclass. Although Taoism esteemed Laozi's *Tao Te Ching*, etc. as its scriptures, it had not formed a system of religious theory and ritual. From the Wei (220-265) and Jin (265-420) dynasties, Taoism gradually split into two factions: one faction was the prayer camp, who adhered to incanted water treatment, spreading through the underclass. The other faction was alchemy, mainly followed by scholars, who used "pills of immortality" and short-term fasting as their main methods of self-cultiva-

Zhang Daoling, a Taoist master of the Tao of the Five-*Dou*-of-Rice

tion. They pursued longevity and immortality, and a change into gods. Alchemy was consistent with the needs of the upper class, among whom Taoism had started its dissemination. Gradually emerging from its initial confrontation with the official position, Taoism became an official religion.

In the Southern and Northern Dynasties (420-581), accompanied by social turmoil and competition between various schools, Taoism had entered a stage of comprehensive development, many Taoist thinkers emerged. They compiled a large number of classics and established a complete religious system comparable with Confucianism and Buddhism, and became an important component of China's traditional culture.

After the establishment of the Tang Dynasty (618-907), they revered Laozi (Li Dan) as their first ancestor. They supported Taoism vigorously, prescribing that it must be above Buddhism. Taoism quickly developed all over the country. Except for Empress Wu Zetian, the majority of the Tang Dynasty emperors and many in the upper classes believed in Taoism.

Taoism continued to blossom during the Song (960-1279) and Yuan (1279-1368) dynasties. On one hand, its different sects gradually converged into the Tao of Zheng Yi in the Yuan Dynasty, giving priority to magic figures and incantations. The Tao of Zheng Yi worshiped demons, and its main activity was to drive off demons and subdue evil spirits, pray for blessings and avert disasters by means of drawing magic figures and chanting incanta-

A Taoist

tions. It was based on superstition, and its monks were also allowed to get married.

On the other hand, there emerged some new sects, the most important of which was called the Tao of Quan Zhen, which advocated the unity of the three religions—Confucianism, Buddhism and Taoism. It revered one scripture out of each religion, and did not engage in drawing magic figures or chanting incantations; instead, it advocated to remove sexual passion, form a peaceful mind through which to return to original purity and simplicity, and later to achieve immortality. Its practitioners have to become a monk or nun.

Genghis Khan had summoned the then leader of the Tao of Quan Zhen, Qiu Chuji. Despite the fact that he was more than 70 years old, Qui Chuji overcame the harshness of the vast Gobi Desert and snow-capped mountains, traveling to Genghis Khan's camp in what is now Afghanistan. When Genghis Khan asked him about his methods of longevity, Qiu Chuji told him not to carry out mass killings; this gained him the respect of Genghis Khan, who called him a God, and allowed him to nurture Taoism. The Tao of Quan Zhen was thus given a great boost, and together with the Tao of Zheng Yi, it became one of the two major factions of late Taoism. The

Qiu Chuji, a Taoist of the Tao of Quan Zhen in the Jin Dynasty.

place where Qiu Chuji passed away—Baiyunguan (first built in the Tang Dynasty)—is the largest Taoist temple in Beijing, and it is also where the China Taoist Association is located.

Each religion has different sects and doctrines. The main Taoist teachings believe in the existence of God, the availability of God, believe that through some form of practice, the followers can ward off illness, achieve longevity and immortality, become gods, and soar into the Heaven. It worships hundreds of gods. Clearly, Taoism is a multi-god religion.

The Taoist magical arts are numerous, and include:

Alchemy. The main materials used in alchemy are five metals, Eight mineral (various minerals and drugs), San Huang (sulphur, realgar, orpiment), mercury, saltpeter, etc. The so-called magical pills refined out of these have great toxicity; they do not cure illnesses or ensure physical fitness, and are injurious to health. Some people even died of barbiturate poisoning. However, the science of alchemy pioneered China's chemical history; the invention of gunpowder can be attributed directly to alchemy.

Various health-enhancing methods, exercises for physical fitness and longevity. These methods are miscellaneous, and some are even absurd, but others are effective—sitting quietly, short-term fasting, meditation, *Qigong*, prescription herbs, etc. They are beneficial physically and mentally, and are still loved and used by people; they possess Chinese characteristics, and as such are worthy of serious study and application.

Divination, occultism, etc. The Taoists used these methods to cure people and ward off disasters. Today, these are seen as merely superstitious tricks; the Taoist priests who employ them do not necessarily believe that they are efficacious, but a way of simply making a living, even if it means cheating people out of their money.

Records of Taoist magic figures

It seems today that the Taoist pursuit of immortality is delusive. Some of the magic arts and prescriptions aimed at this are absurd, but Taoism still pursue longevity as much as it can, cherishes life, enjoys life, and advocates that one's life is determined by oneself rather than God. Moreover, in the process, it explores methods that are beneficial to the treatment of diseases and the promotion of fitness, contributing to overall health of humanity.

3. The Introduction of Buddhism and Islam

Buddhism

In the case of China, Buddhism is an alien religion. It was founded by Siddhartha Gautama, Prince of the ancient Indian city Kapilavastu (in the south of Nepal today) between 6th and 5th century BC (at the time of China's Spring and Autumn and Warring States periods).

It is difficult to determine the exact time when Buddhism came to China. A story goes like this: Emperor Ming of the Eastern Han Dynasty (reigning from 58 to 75) dreamed one night of a golden figure flying over the palace. The next day he asked his ministers what this meant, and one of them explained that it was the "Buddha". Emperor Ming sent people to Auckland (now India) to search for Buddhist doctrines. Accompanied by two Indian monks, they carried a statue of Buddha and Buddhist scriptures back to Luoyang, with a white horse. In Luoyang they established China's first official Buddhist temple—the White Horse Temple. It is generally believed that Buddhism came into China during the period between the Western Han Dynasty (206 BC-AD 25) and the Eastern Han Dynasty (25-220). From the end of the Eastern Han Dynasty, social unrest led to divergences in people's thinking. Buddhism became more and more popular. During the Southern and Northern Dynasties (420-581), it saw comprehensive and sustained development—a great number of temples were constructed, with numerous monks in each. Emperor Wu (Xiao Yan) of the State of Liang of the Southern Dynasties (502-557), in particular, respected Buddhism. In order to express his piety, he sacrificed himself four successive times as a "slave" in various temples, and the country had to spend a huge amount of money buying back his freedom. He also built numerous Buddhist monasteries, and set down the Chinese Buddhist prohibition of meat-eating as well. These practices promoted the further spread of Buddhism. During the Sui (581-618) and Tang (618-907) dynasties, with the country unified, most of the rulers vigorously promoted Buddhism, and Buddhism reached its peak.

What is particularly worth mentioning here is the relationship between Buddhism and the only female emperor in Chinese history, Wu Zetian (reigning from 690 to 705). She had once been one of the many concubines of the emperor, but had a strong desire for power; after a bitter court fight, she became empress. After the death of the emperor, she went as far as wanting to be emperor herself. This had never happened before in China's history, and it did not agree with China's political and cultural traditions. Therefore, it got no support from the Taoist or Confucian cultural traditions. Buddhist scriptures, however, testified that a female body became the King of Spinning Wheel and later a Buddha, so she resorted to Buddhism. At the time, a monk wrote a timely passage named "*Great Cloud Sutra*" and dedicated it to her, claiming that she was a Western Maitreya who had descended on the world, and that she should become leader of the country. Wu Zetian gladly accepted the statement and immediately ordered the "*Great Cloud Sutra*" be issued all over the country. She conveniently mounted the throne of the emperor, considering herself to be Maitreya, and granted herself a title with strong Buddhist overtones—Golden-Wheel Sacred Emperor. Earlier, as in the Tang Dynasty, the emperors' family name was Li (the same as Laozi's); they respected Laozi and preferred Taoism to Buddhism. Wu Zetian then publicly announced Buddhism's superiority over Taoism, and held two large-scale activities to welcome the Sarira, which was enshrined in Famen Temple. She also bestowed a large number of exquisite artifacts on Famen Temple. Exhibited in Famen Temple Museum of Shaanxi Province, these objects are now part of China's precious heritage. The era of Wu Zetian witnessed the great development of China's Buddhism.

Buddhist theories flourished during the Tang Dynasty. Famous monk Xuan Zang (602-664) experienced untold hardships for 19 years; he went to faraway India to study Buddhist sutras. After returning, he took charge of the translation of 75 Buddhist scriptures, 1,335 volumes in all. Well-known monks came forth in great numbers. They carried out in-depth research and profound expositions of Buddhist doctrines and theories, and integrated them into Confucian ethical concepts and Taoist thinking. Buddhist theories and sects were thus formed with China's national characteristics, and included *Tiantai*, Dharmalaksana, Avatamsaka, *Zen*, Pure Land and so on. With the popularity of the Buddhist faith, Buddhist architecture, sculpture, painting, music, etc., with their unique characteristics, came into being as well, greatly enriching the cultural and artistic treasury of China. Later, based on the story of Xuan Zang's pilgrimage to faraway India for Buddhist scriptures, novelist Wu Cheng'en wrote the mythic novel *Journey to the West*. In it, the Tang Monk and his three disciples conquer

Buddhas, a Tangka painting from the Tashilunpo Monastery, Xigaze, Tibet Autonomous Region, Qing Dynasty

devils and monsters all along the way, becoming legendary figures who go through thick and thin for the sake of truth. The story of *Journey to the West* is well known among young and old, and has been eulogized everywhere for generations. It has become one of China's four famous literary classics; its spirit has inspired the Chinese people to work hard, and forge ahead. With the Tang Dynasty's power and frequent exchanges between China and foreign countries, Chinese Buddhism also spread to Japan, Korea, Vietnam, Indonesia and other neighboring countries. Monk Jianzhen of Daming Temple in Yangzhou surmounted numerous difficulties, sailing east to Japan to spread Buddhism. His deeds became a much-told story in the history of Sino-Japanese cultural exchanges. (See Chapter 8)

Tang monk Xuan Zang and his three disciples on their journey to the west to acquire Buddhist scriptures

In the same period of the Sui and Tang dynasties, Tibetan Buddhism was founded. This was another great achievement for Chinese Buddhism. In the 7th century, Songtsan Gambo unified the Tibetan Plateau, established the famous Tubo Kingdom, formed connections through marriages with Nepal and the Tang Dynasty, and introduced Buddhism. With the support of the past Tibetan kings, Buddhism rapidly spread in the Tibetan regions, gradually forming Tibetan Buddhism with local characteristics— Lamaism. In the Yuan Dynasty (1279-1368), Tibet was incorporated into Chinese territory, and a unified system of politics and religion was established. Lamaism was like the Catholic Church in Europe of the Middle Ages, having a very significant impact upon the political and social life of the Tibetans.

The Mogao Grottoes, Dunhuang, Gansu Province

The Yungang Grottoes, Datong, Shanxi Province

Buddhism had a profound impact on Chinese culture and life, and infiltrated into Chinese philosophy, ethics, literature, art, architecture, music, as well as people's daily lives. Buddhist doctrines of various sects had a major impact on the development of China's academic thinking. Karmic philosophy penetrated the Chinese people's psyche and cultivated the concepts and conducts of doing good. With respect to literature, many works chose the theme of karma, how being good or bad influenced one's future lives.

Lots of expressions in the Chinese vocabulary also were from Buddhism, including terms such as "the world", "truthfully", "equality", "instant", "regulations, taboos and commandments", "absolute", "relative", and so on. Buddhist temples have existed throughout various parts of China, in urban and rural areas,

The Longmen Grottoes, Luoyang, Henan Province

and in remote mountains. Even today, if we travel in China, we find many places of interest and historic sites closely related to Buddhism.

Chinese Buddhism left a rich cultural heritage, most notably the four famous mountains and the grottoes. The four famous mountains are the Wutai Mountain in Shanxi Province, Mount Emei in Sichuan Province, Jiuhua Mountain in Anhui Province and Putuo Mountain in Zhejiang Province. People enshrine and worship a different Buddha in each place, where there is a wide variety of Buddhist architecture and beautiful scenery. The four grottoes are the Mogao Grottoes located in Dunhuang, Gansu Province, the Yungang Grottoes in Datong in Shanxi Province, the Longmen Grottoes in Luoyang, Henan Province, and the Maiji Mountain Grottoes in Tianshui, Gansu Province. Among them, the Dunhuang Mogao Grottos (also called Thousand-Buddha Caves) on the Silk Road is world-renowned. Its carving began at the beginning of the 4th century, and after about 1,000 years of continuous operation, it left behind a large number of exquisite frescos and statues, Buddhist scrolls and secular literature. It is the world's largest Buddhist art treasury in existence. Many of the Buddhist scrolls, and even some frescos and statues, were gradually looted one after another by the so-called "adventurers" from Britain, France, Russia, Japan, and other countries in the early 20th century. Today, Dunhuang studies have become a global science.

During the spread of Buddhism in China, it also encountered boycotts borne out of political, economic, and cultural factors, but in general, the spread was peaceful. Buddhism and Chinese culture gradually merged, or one could say the original Chinese culture transformed Buddhism, the result being the formation of a Buddhist culture with Chinese characteristics. This became an important part of China's traditional culture.

Islam

Islam is foreign to China as well. It was brought in with the influx of a large number of Muslims, and unlike Buddhism's spread in China, Islam maintained its original identity.

In 651, the Tang Dynasty was in power, and there existed frequent exchanges between China and foreign countries. Rich, prosperous, and populous China attracted a lot of foreign business-people, as well as diplomatic envoys. Mohammed Caliph the Third sent an emissary to China, the first Arab emissary in the country. He went to Chang'an, capital of the Tang Dynasty, and intro-duced to Emperor Gaozong the Arab Empire (the State of Dashi, in Chinese history books) and the teachings of Islam. In general, Chinese historians regard this year as the coming of Islam to China. Since then, friendly contacts between China and the Arab Empire have been increasingly frequent, and the two have established close economic and political relations. According to historical records, during the 140 years of the Tang Dynasty from 651 to 789, the Arab Empire sent envoys to China 39 times, and Persia (now Iran) send 20 envoys to China. At the same time, a large number of Arab and Persian Muslim businesspeople came to China along the Maritime Silk Road. Naturally, they brought Islam to China. Settling down in China, they set up mosques, and established self-governing organizations. With the passage of time, many Arabs and Persians joined the Chinese nationality, becoming the first group of Chinese Muslims.

The large-scale spread of Islam in China was mostly during the Yuan Dynasty (1279-1368). As the Mongolians had established a great empire spanning the Eurasian continent, China and Central Asia for a time linked up as an organic whole. Large quantities of Persians, Arabs and people of every ethnic group in Central Asia left home for China, traveling along the Silk Road. The Muslims coming to China at this period were the most and various in status. In addition to businesspeople, there were a large number of soldiers and artisans who had joined the Mongolian army; there was also a minority of nobles, religious figures, intellectuals, etc., who had attached themselves to the Mongolian regime. They attended the Mongolian military, were assigned throughout the country at garrisons, and later settled in the localities, establishing homes, purchasing goods and building careers. They gradually formed a new national community. Since the Muslims were commonly known as "Hui" in the Yuan Dynasty, this newly formed nationality in China was called the Hui nationality. Later, it was common knowledge that "the Huis of the Yuan Dynasty were all over the world".

The specific historical conditions surrounding this nationality decided that it would be different from other nationalities. It had no fixed residential area; from the Yuan Dynasty to today, the Huis were distributed in various parts of China, focused mainly in northwest China's Ningxia and Gansu, and southwest China's Yunnan. However, they were joined by their common religious belief—Islam.

The spread of Islam in China was relatively slow. The main reason for this was that it did not proselytize, nor did it contend for hegemony with other religions. It was thus not subject to other religions' envy and attacks, but the disadvantage was that people were not aware of its teachings, and naturally it was difficult to spread. However, special geographical and political reasons ensured that it was widely disseminated in China's northwestern regions. The Uygur and other nationalities in today's Xinjiang and Gansu regions formerly believed in Shamanism, Manicheanism, and Buddhism. In the 10th century when Islam spread along the Silk Road, the rulers of this area converted to Islam, and then launched a series of *jihad* (religious wars), spreading Islam by force. Islam was introduced to China in the Yuan Dynasty on a large scale. Several khanates of the Mongol Empire in the Xinjiang region and Central Asia converted to Islam in succession. By the 17th century, Southern Xinjiang had become the domain of Islam. In the 18th century, after the Qing government suppressed a rebellion in Northern Xinjiang, the Muslims migrated to Southern Xinjiang moved to Northern Xinjiang, where gradually became the center of Islam of China. Thus, after about eight centuries, Islam became a major religion, followed by various minorities in the Xinjiang region. Today, China has ten nationalities that have faith in Islam; with the exception of the Hui nationality, the nine live in compact communities in the Xinjiang and Gansu areas.

A mosque in Linxia, Gansu Province

The Niujie Mosque, Beijing

As opposed to Buddhism, China's Islam preserved its original beliefs and rituals; the Muslims in the northwest region maintained their own lifestyles, by and large. However, as China's Islam, it inevitably bore some Chinese characteristics, the most notable being assimilation of the Han language, in particular by the Hui scattered in various parts of China. Islamic teachings needed to be expressed in Chinese. They chose the words "clear", "real", "clean", "pure" and so on to show that Islam bore the characteristics of purity, and gradually fixed on the two Chinese characters *Qing* and *Zhen* (namely "clear" and "real"). The place of worship was called *Qingzhen* Temple (mosque).

Well-known mosques include Niujie Mosque in Beijing,

Aitiga Mosque in Xinjiang, Dongguan Grand Mosque in Xining, Qinghai Province, Nanguan Mosque in Yinchuan, Ningxia Hui Autonomous Region, Dongdasi Mosque in Kaifeng, Henan Province, and so on. Restaurants running in accordance with Islamic dietary habits are called *Qingzhen* restaurants (Muslim restaurants). Other matters related to Islam are generally linked with the two Chinese characters *Qing* and *Zhen*. Apart from the fact that they do not eat pork, the Huis, scattered in the urban and rural areas of inland China, have no obvious differences in living habits. The most marked characteristic of Islamic dietary habits is that they do not eat pork.

Clearly, a notable feature of the Chinese people's religious concepts is religious tolerance and peaceful coexistence. Even more interesting is that from the beginning of the Tang and Song dynasties, a tendency had developed for the three religions— Confucianism, Buddhism, and Taoism—to unite, especially when the Taoist Quanzhen Sect openly declared that its doctrines were the unity of the three religions. Since then, Confucianism, Buddhism, and Taoism interacted and merged. In some religious architecture, the three gods are worshiped at the same time, although each has his own characteristics. Moreover, the overwhelming majority of the ordinary Chinese people, who were not specifically religious clergy—from the well-educated bureaucratic literati to illiterate commoners—believed in Confucianism, Buddhism, and Taoism at the same time. In the mythic novel *Journey to the West*, among the gods in Heaven, the Jade Emperor, *Tai Shang Lao Jun* (Lord the Most High, respectful form of address for Laozi by Taoists), and so on were Taoist figures, while the Goddess of Mercy was a Buddhist figure. When the Monkey King made trouble in Heaven, the Jade Emperor did not know what to do, so at last he resorted to the Western Tathagata Buddha, who tamed the monkey. Such situations where various religions integrate and cooperate rarely occur in other parts of the world. In China, not only are there no religious wars, but there are few conflicts between religions, possibly due to the unique inclusive spirit of the Chinese people.

Chapter 7

Dawn of Civilization

Chinese civilization has a history of over 5,000 years, its development vital and continuous since ancient times. In the course of the country's long history, the Chinese people produced a splendid civilization that covered politics, economy, military, education, philosophy, religion, arts, science and technology, and so forth. Some of these have distinct national characteristics, still others have made important contributions to human civilization as a whole. Here, we select a few fragments to be introduced briefly. The Four Great Inventions—papermaking, printing, gunpowder and the compass—were great contributions by China to humankind. The Chinese imperial examination system was a unique system of selecting officials. In addition, this terse write-up about ancient Chinese literature, calligraphy, painting, architecture and so on can give readers a glimpse into China's unique artistic styles.

1. The Four Great Inventions

The papermaking technique, printing, gunpowder, and compass—the so-called Four Great Inventions—had far-reaching historic significance, for they changed human life once and for all. The British philosopher Francis Bacon observed in 1962 that printing, gunpowder, and compass, the three inventions that were "unknown to the ancients", had in his day "changed the whole face and state of things through the whole world: first in literature, second in warfare, third in navigation; whence have followed innumerable changes, in so much that no empire, no sect, no star seems to have exerted greater power and influence in human affairs than these mechanical discoveries." Karl Marx said, "Chinese gunpowder blew the feudal class of knights to smithereens; the compass opened up world markets and built colonies; and printing became an implement of Protestantism and the most powerful lever and necessary precondition for intellectual development and creation."

Neither mentioned papermaking specifically—not that they considered it unimportant, but that it was only naturally regarded as a prerequisite to the development and widespread use of printing. Of course, China's contribution to mankind was by no means confined simply to science and technology, in the same way as China's ancient inventions were not limited only to the four great inventions. As the famous British scientific historian Joseph Needham pointed out, in his monumental work *Science and Civilization in China*, "there were more" and the Four Great Inventions were nothing less than outstanding representatives of the large number of scientific and technological achievements by the ancient Chinese, representing an "oversimplification". Paper was invented in the Han Dynasty (206 BC-AD 220), block-printing and gunpowder in the Tang Dynasty (618-907) and compass and movable-type printing in the Song Dynasty (960-1279); the earlier ones date back about 2,000 years, and even the later ones have a history of nearly 1,000 years. Now, let's take the Four Great Inventions one by one.

Papermaking

As human civilization progressed, there came the need to keep a record either through pictures or writing, both of which called for some material to depend on. Today, there are all kinds of paper available, in addition to PCs, video cameras, and other advanced equipment, which enable us to record whatever we want with more efficiency and convenience which were our ancestors denied.

Early people tried different kinds of recording materials. Hieroglyphics—pictures reflecting the lives of the ancients—have been discovered on the walls of stone caves all over the world. It is most likely that stone cave walls are the first recording materials ever preserved so far. In the two river valleys of Tigris and Euphrates, people turned fine clay into mud by mixing it with water, then molded it into boards and, in the end, dried the boards in the open for writing. Perhaps, it was because people wrote (or carved, if you like) on those clay boards with pointed wooden rods or sticks and, as a result, the strokes of the characters were thick at the one end and thin at the other like a wedge, that the scripts are known as cuneiform or sphenogram.

Mud plate and mud cover carved fully with arrow headed characters

In ancient Egypt, people used papyrus as material. The English word *paper*, French word *papier*, and Spanish word *papel* all come from 'papyrus'. People split the pith in the stalk of papyrus into thin strips, overlapped one on another, and then, after drying, polishing and trimming, a finished product of paper took shape. This paper was brought to Europe later on, and became widely used by Mediterranean people. In the 2nd century BC, because Egypt banned the export of papyrus, Europeans changed over to parchment—paper made of leather (sheepskin enduring for the most part). There were quite a few procedures in making parchment. Soft, enduring and easy to write on, parchment, which was invented in the Greek city state Pergamum (on a river bank of present-day Turkey), was all the rage for a while since the 3rd century, and it did not step down from the stages of history until the 13th century. In ancient India, people turned the broad leaf of the palm into writing material. Palms are called *pattra* in India. Because the Indians wrote a lot of Buddhist sutra on the palm leaf, it became synonymous with Buddhist Scripture. Buddhism exerted a tremendous influence on Chinese culture, which probably explains why we continue to use the word leaf when talking about book pages up to now.

In ancient China, people made use of many different materials for recording. There were pictures, characters and scripts painted or drawn on the potteries of the Yangshao Culture (about 5000-3000 BC). In the Shang Dynasty (*c.*1600-1046 BC), people carved on the bones of beasts and shells of tortoises; these are known as oracle-bone inscriptions. The Western Zhou people (*c.*1100-771 BC) engraved characters on bronze vessels. During the Spring and Autumn and the Warring States periods (770-221 BC), inscribed bamboo strips, wooden tablets, and silk were significant. Bamboo and wood were at once easy to get and easy to write on, so they were widely employed as writing materials. However, when there was much to write down, large numbers of bamboo strips and wooden tablets had to be strung up together, and this made the books cumbersome to carry or even read. In comparison, silk was much easier to handle, but it was too expensive to popularize.

As the Han Dynasty (206-220 BC) came on, the economy showed signs of prosperity, and so did culture and education. Emperor Wu of the Han Dynasty (140-88 BC) attached much importance to Confucianism and set off a surge of Confucian study. By that time, neither cumbersome bamboo strips and wooden tablets, nor expensive silk, could meet the need. Search for a new material started, and papermaking techniques soon emerged as a result.

According to archeological findings, paper first appeared in the Western Han Dynasty (206 BC-AD 25) in China. Although there is academic controversy about it, at least one thing is certain: there appeared something like paper in the Western Han Dynasty. Of course, the "paper" of the time was sure to be of low quality and output, and was not widely used.

It is generally acknowledged that papermaking was invented by the eunuch Cai Lun in the Eastern Han Dynasty (25-220), or at least it's safe to say that he made the most significant improvement to it.

Cai Lun

Cai Lun, born in 63 AD, was forced to go to the imperial palace and became a eunuch at the age of 13. There he received some basic education and training in protocol. With his quick mind and diligence, he soon distinguished himself from his group and became the head. After a few years, he was sent to wait on the crown prince, Liu Zhao. They got along well. When Liu Zhao, later Emperor He of the Han Dynasty (89-105), ascended the throne, he paid due respect to Cai Lun and reserved important positions for him.

The empress was fond of scribbling

and drawing with Chinese ink on paper, and Cai Lun displayed his talent for making things, so in 92 AD he was appointed as Shangfang Ling. Shangfang was the government office in charge of the making of imperial weaponry, like sabers, swords, etc., as well as utensils and playthings for the emperor. Ling was head of the office. During the term of his office, Cai Lun paid special attention to innovations of the papermaking technique on the basis of what had been achieved since the Western Han Dynasty.

With repeated close observation, field investigations and assiduous experiments and practices, he finally came up with a new method of papermaking. On one hand, he adopted new materials: bark, bits of rope, rags, worn-out fishnets, and the fabrics of hemp and flax. By doing so, he could kill many birds with one stone: convert waste into useful materials, open up new sources, bring down the cost, and increase the production of paper. On the other hand, there was the improvement in the technological level, which was crucial to making paper of high quality, especially the use of multiple materials, which entailed more sophisticated techniques. Cai Lun managed to solve the major problems in papermaking, and finalized the procedures for the production of paper: *Ou* (to soak the material up), *Cuo* (to cut the material into pieces), *Zhu* (to steam and boil the material), *Dao* (to beat), *Chao* (to scoop and strain), *Shai* (to dry). Among the procedures, beating was the key link, and by steaming and boiling in basified liquid of lime white, the fabric of the plant became even finer, and thus the quality of paper was greatly enhanced.

In 105, Cai Lun reported his achievement to the royal court and won the approval of both the emperor and the empress. With the popularization of his paper, he was granted the title of Marquis Longting (with the conferred fief in today's Yangxian County, Shaanxi Province), and people named his paper after his title—

Cai Lun making paper

Caihou Paper (Marquis Cai's paper). With its popularization, paper replaced bamboo strips, wooden tablets and silk as the major recording material. Since then, every generation and dynasty saw new development and advancements in the papermaking technique, and consequently, paper became better in quality, richer in variety, and more and more extensive in use.

Paper has a clear superiority over other recording materials, and for this reason, it caught on rapidly with other countries as well. At the end of the 4th century, papermaking techniques reached the Korean Peninsula. And through technological innovation, Korean papermaking craftsmen made a kind of paper which was even smoother, cleaner and more enduring. The paper was sold back to China afterwards and known to the Chinese as Korean paper. Papermaking techniques were introduced to Japan in the 7th century and to the Arabic Empire in the 8th century, from where it was passed further west to Europe and south to Africa. By the Renaissance, every major European country had built a workshop or two for papermaking. In 1690, the first paper mill of America was set up in Philadelphia, and in 1868, Australia established a paper mill in the vicinity of Melbourne. So far, China's papermaking technique had found its way to every corner of the world, making tremendous contributions to communication between countries. People all over the world acknowledged what the Chinese people had done for mankind, especially what was achieved by Cai Lun. In America, France, Japan, and many other countries, people built memorial halls for Cai Lun. In November 2007, The *Time magazine* released a list of the best inventors in history, Cai Lun ranked high among the great names.

The Printing Technique

Before the invention of printing, the circulation of knowledge was done mainly by making private hand-copies, at once time-consuming and unreliable. At the beginning of the 6th century (somewhere between the Sui (581-618) and Tang (618-907) dynasties, with advances in papermaking, printing rose to the occasion with the popularizing of seals, signets, stamps, chops, and rubbings of texts from stone tablets. Block printing was first. In block printing, people first carved reversed characters or drawings on a block of wooden board, and then pasted Chinese ink on it to print them on paper; next, people fastened the printed pages together, enclosed them in a protective cover; lastly, a volume came into being. It was an epoch-making invention: the era of hand-copying ended and a new era of printing was ushered in. The invention was first applied to the printing of images of the Buddha, Buddhist Scriptures, poetry anthologies, calendars and almanacs, etc.

However, there is an intrinsic drawback in block printing—every page of a book must be engraved on a printing block and when there is a minor error on it, the whole block has to be discarded. This gave rise to high costs. Later on, by introducing a movable type of printing, Bi Sheng solved the problem beautifully.

Bi Sheng (?-1051) was an ordinary printer who used his brains well in practical work. History held that, one day, he happened to see his two sons playing games with clay. They made toy pots, bowls, tables, pigs, and other figures out of clay, and displayed them this way and that as they pleased. Bi Sheng had an inspiration at once: if he engraved every single character on a seal, then they could be arranged in such a way as was required. With the idea, he invented movable types. A scientist of the Northern Song Dynasty (960-1127), Shen Kuo (1031-1095), recorded the invention in great detail in his big book, *Dream Pool Essays*.

According to the book, Bi Sheng carved characters on clay seals one by one, one seal for one character, and hardened the clay seals in a fire. He prepared an iron board in advance and laid rosin, wax and paper ash on it. Then he used an iron frame to get the board fixed on all four sides and set clay seals in the frame. A whole-packed board made a printing plate or a block. Next, by heating the plate on fire, he melted the rosin and wax to stick the seals to the plate. Finally, after he had leveled the seals with another flat board, the block was ready for printing. In order to raise efficiency, two plates were used at the same time: when one was in printing, the other was under preparation; when one was finished with printing, the other was ready to go. So by using two plates in an alternative way, printing went on faster. For each character, several spare seals were prepared, and for each of those general service characters, as many as 20 seals were made to provide against repeats of certain characters within a block. When not in use, they were kept in store in wooden boxes in alphabetic order. As for those rarely used characters, no ready-made seals were in hand, so people had to improvise at the last minute— they carved the characters on seals and hardened them in fire. The reason why clay was employed instead of wood was simply that wood was easy to go out of form with water and difficult to remove from the sticky staff on the board, unlike clay, which could be easily taken off the board and thrown into another use in no time.

The method displayed no overwhelming superiority in printing a small number of books, like two or three books, but when it came to the printing of a large number of books, hundreds or thousands of books, for instance, it had no equal. Moreover, when any mistake occurred in the printing, a remedy could be made easily and rapidly. For instance, it once took a lot of people a lot of time to carve as many as 130,000 wooden blocks in order to print the more than 5,000 volumes of the *Tripitaka*. If the movable type of printing had been used, the job would have been done in no more than two months. In 2006, type-printed Buddhist scriptures were discovered in China's Ningxia Hui Autonomous Region—*A Collection of Summary Annotations of the Excellent Lotus Sutra*, of the Western Xia Period (1038-1227). This is the earliest type of presswork found in the world so far.

The movable type of printing went through several improvements later on. Metal and non-metal materials, which were, needless to say, much stronger and more endurable, were substituted for clay. Through diplomatic envoys and businessmen, the new improved technique was brought to Korea, Japan, Southeast Asia and Europe, until its influence reached every corner of the world.

The invention of the movable type of printing may well be called a revolution in printing history. It was another great contribution that China had made to the development of world civilization.

Gunpowder

Different from papermaking and printing, which were invented with a clear aim, *Huo Yao*—which literally means "inflammable medicine" in Chinese—was acquired quite accidentally by the ancient Chinese alchemists. What ancient Chinese alchemists aimed at was not gold actually, but a medicine in the shape of red pills, which promised longevity, or even immortality. Cinnabar was found to be the main composition of *Dan* (the longevity pills). Though ancient Chinese alchemists ended up with different materials in the making of *Dan*, they happened to agree on the method by which *Dan* ought to be produced: mixing the materials in proper proportion first and then smelting them in a pot on fire. Gunpowder was obtained quite by chance in that process. Some of the common materials for the making of *Dan* were the five metals, eight minerals, three yellow materials: sulphur, red orpiment, and citrine orpiment, mercury and niter. Of these, niter, the main composition of gunpowder, was an oxidizer, and would explode when heated up together with the three *Huangs*. And so, the invention of gunpowder was a natural follow-up.

Chinese alchemy dates back to the Western Han Dynasty. Compatibility from *The Perspective of the Book of Changes*, written by the Eastern Han alchemist, Wei Boyang, was acknowledged as the first monograph on *Dan* in the world. He used jargons such as *yin* and *yang*, *ci* and *xiong* (two pairs of opposing principles in nature, the former of each pair feminine and negative, the latter masculine and positive, as often seen in Chinese philosophy, medicine, etc.), to expound on the corresponding activities of several materials in the mixture. Moreover, he pointed out three phenomena: first, when the *ci* materials met with the *xiong*, everything (the making of pills of immortality) went on smoothly. Second, when two *Ci* materials met, as if—as the author put it— two girls were put under the same roof, nothing would happen and no fruit would be borne. Third, when the *xiong* materials of different categories were put together with no consideration of their respective special property, that is to say, when *xiong* materials of different types and amounts met in one formula, an explosion was sure to happen. Anyway, as we can see from above, the emergence of gunpowder happened no later than the Eastern Han Dynasty.

At first gunpowder was used for magic or playing tricks on people. Later on, it was gradually brought into military use. Records show that in the Three Kingdoms period (220-280), a war between the Shu and Wei broke out and the army of Wei beat that of Shu in the end, by firing stones at the enemy. Another record says that the army of Wei shot "fire arrows" at the scaling ladders of the army of Shu, set them on fire and burnt the enemy to death. No matter what weapons they were, the fact was as clear as day that gunpowder had been made for military use.

In the Song Dynasty (960-1279), the continual wars between the central government and the minorities accelerated the development and widespread use of gunpowder. The government set up special institutions for the manufacturing of gunpowder and corresponding weapons—incendiary weapons such as gunpowder-propelled arrows and fire arrows; and explosive weapons, such as the Thunderbolt Canon (a primitive gun) and the heaven-shaking mine (a primitive explosive). In 1259, the Southern Song Dynasty invented the firelock, a gun with gunpowder stuffed in a long bamboo barrel and small shot as ammunition. It was claimed to be the first barrel-shaped firearm ever known in China, marking the biggest step forward in firearm history. When the Yuan Dynasty (1279-1368) came on, the bronze blunderbuss, also called General Bronze (its Chinese nickname), appeared. All the above-mentioned weapons took advantage of the combustible power of gunpowder to eject a destructive projectile, manifesting unprecedented power.

In China, another big use was bestowed on

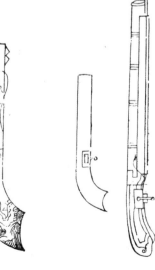

Detailed patterns of firelocks

gunpowder in the making of firecrackers and fireworks, which had become an inalienable part of festival celebrations and other occasions. In the 12th and 13th centuries, gunpowder was brought to Arabic countries, then to Greek and Europe. Gunpowder changed both weapons and the modes of war once and for all. Besides, gunpowder has since been widely used by people in productive and economic activities, accelerating the advancement of human society.

The Compass

As early as in the Warring States Period (475-221 BC), Chinese people chanced upon the property of a natural magnetite: to attract iron and point fixedly north. After constant improvement, a ladle-shaped primitive "south-pointer" came into being, this one being round at the bottom and well-balanced as a whole. When placed on a slippery plate, it started out revolving automatically and horizontally, and when it finally came to a standstill, the handle of the ladle pointed to the south.

With repeated close observations and experiments, people learnt that magnetic stones drew iron rather than other metals or non-metals. This discovery spurred people to devise a way to magnetize a piece of iron and replace magnetic stones with magnetic iron. By the Jin Dynasty (265-420), people had learnt to make south-pointing fish out of magnetic iron. In the Song Dynasty (960-1279), people mastered the technique of magnetizing something in an artificial way, which led to the first compass.

In the Northern Song Dynasty (960-1127), Zeng Gongliang (999-1078)

A compass

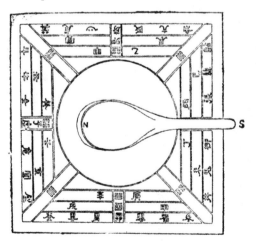

wrote in *Collection of the Most Important Military Techniques* details of how to make and employ a south-pointing fish. His idea was to take advantage of the magnetic field of the earth and make a piece of iron magnetic. He held a piece of red heated fish-shaped iron in the meridian line orientation, because the iron molecules were in a much more active state when heated, and arranged them-selves in the direction of the magnetic field of the earth. By dipping the hot iron into the water, he cooled the fish off and fixed the interior arrangement of the molecules rapidly. A little later, Shen Kuo recorded in his *Dream Pool Essays* another method of magnetization: rub an iron needle against a magnetite, and with the aid of the magnetic field of a naturally magnetic stone, the arrangement of the interior magnetic flux tends to be in one direction, thus magnetizing the iron needle. This method is not only simple but more effective. In addition, it was at this time that the Chinese discovered declination, about 400 years earlier than Colombo did in 1493 (the two magnetic poles of the earth do not equate with the geographical north and south pole, and the magnetic needle points to the magnetic poles, not the geographical poles of the earth; therefore, the magnetic needle does not point to the true north or the true south, but slightly declines; the angle between the direction of the magnetic needle and the true north or south is declination).

A military compass of the Three Kingdoms period (model)

The invention of man-made magnetite was a milestone in the development of the compass. In order to indicate direction accu-rately, apart from the necessary south-pointing needle, there was yet another requisite for the completion of a compass—*Luopan*, a device used to determine geographic direction, usually consisting of a round disc which was equally divided into 24 sections, each marking a different direction. *Luopan* appeared no later than the Southern Song Dynasty (1127-1279). By looking at the needle, people could distinguish which direction they were going.

The compass was first used to practice *Fengshui* (geomancy), for superstitious people believed that the location of a house, grave, etc., from the perspective of the geomantic features of surroundings and nearby hills and waters, affected the fortunes of a family and its descendants. Later the use of the compass spread to other aspects of our lives, and it was especially useful for navigation purposes. In the Song Dynasty, the application of the compass in navigation was confined only to bad weather, say, on cloudy days. On a fine day, people would "watch stars at night and look at the sun by day". By the Yuan Dynasty (1279-1368), the compass had become the most important direction-finding equipment at sea. Whatever the weather, the compass could be used to navigate the ship. The compass allowed men all-weather capability in navigation and opened a new era in history. It was owing to the application of the compass, plus the advancement of other navigation techniques, that Zheng He in the Ming Dynasty (1368-1644) could sail as far as the Atlantic Ocean (See Chapter 8)—a magnificent Chinese feat in the history of navigation.

At about the end of the 12th century and the beginning of the 13th, the Arab countries began to learn how to make the compass, and later it traversed the Arab world to Europe. The spread of the compass to Europe opened the oceans of the world for travel, and led to the discovery of the New World and the realization of round-the-globe tours. The subsequent change in the setup of the world became inevitable.

2. The Imperial Examination System

The imperial examination system was the means by which Chinese feudal dynasties selected competent candidates for civil and military posts. Spanning the Sui (581-618) to Qing (1644-1911) dynasties, the imperial examination system existed for 1,300 years in Chinese history. Before the emergence of the imperial examination system, there existed in Chinese history the system of enfeoffment of the Western Zhou Dynasty (c.1100-771 BC) in the pre-Qin period (before 221 BC), the appointing system of the Han Dynasty (206 BC-AD 220), the nine-grade official system of the Wei and Jin periods (220-420), etc., all of which were used to select men of talent for office. A ruler granted fief and hereditary titles to the imperial kinsmen and the nobility, who then further conferred them upon their vassals. The royal member or the noble was the governor of his territories and was responsible for their administration. And what was more important, he had to serve the ruler. By the appointing system, the incumbent officials made investigatory trips to find skilled men, and would then recommend them to the central government. After the evaluation of their qualifications, these men would be entrusted with government posts.

However, inherent evils within the system revealed themselves, and as a result, some incompetent people were put in important positions. The nine-grade official system, also known as the dominant family system, ran like this: first, some locals who enjoyed great prestige were elected as the impartial officials in the locality; then, it was up to them to pass judgment on the qualified personnel in the area under their jurisdiction, and divide them into nine grades according to their ability and the established criteria; lastly, the government chose proper people for proper positions according to their respective grades. However, in practice, people of talent were classified and appointed by their family status, not by their merit and ability. Under the system, people of ability but not of high status had no chance of getting promoted, which caused enormous waste of talent. In fact, it did not bring any good to the stability of society or benefit the ruling class.

The Sui Dynasty began the practice of recruiting talents through examinations. Although the system of examinations left much to be desired, the spirit embodied in the established principles of the practice was no doubt a great advancement: without consideration of status, regardless of their noble or humble origins, examinees competed against each other on equal terms and were given employment or rejected according to their scores, that is, their abilities. The practice made certain that state power was opened to all social strata, thus preventing the real talents from being stifled. Also it reinforced the foundations of the ruling class and helped the stability and advancement of the society. The chosen officials had a relatively high standard of education and overall skill levels. Therefore, the following dynasties continued to use the system, and made their own additions and deletions to specific rules and regulations. By the Ming (1368-1644) and Qing (1644-1911) dynasties a complete, well-organized system of examinations had taken shape. In fact, the imperial examination was a crucial means for the ruler to build his pool of talents, and consolidate his rule.

The imperial examination was graded written examinations. Before taking part, the candidates had to pass qualifying examinations, which were presided over by the local governor. The survivors were entitled *Xiucai*, i.e. a licentiate. The formal examinations, which were held every three years, were separated into three grades. The first grade of examination was provincial, held in the provincial capital in autumn and presided over by imperial envoys—a chief invigilator (examiner) and a vice invigilator. The survivors on this level were entitled *Juren*. The second year after the provincial examination, in the spring, all the *Juren* went to the state capital to take national examination, which was organized by the Ministry of Rites (the office that was in charge of the selection and promotion of officials in feudal China). The survivors were *Gongshi*. After the national examination, there followed the palace examination,

Scholars participating in the imperial examination

which, as its name implied, was presided over by the emperor, in person. The successes were *Jinshi*, and the one who came first was *Zhuangyuan*, the Number One Scholar. The examination was closely overseen and strict rules were laid down for marking the examination papers. After the examinee passed the imperial examination at the county level and became a *Xiucai*, he acquired a degree of prestige, but only when he succeeded in the palace examination could he be qualified for an official position. The first three in the palace examination were directly assigned posts in Hanlinyuan, the Imperial Academy. The others had to take one more examination; those who distinguished themselves were given the opportunity to study in Hanlinyuan; the others were assigned posts in the central government or local governments. The lucky ones in Hanlinyuan were faced with yet another examination in three years, after which the distinguished ones held posts in Hanlinyuan, while the others went to work in the ministries or local governments. Hanlinyuan was an important office, responsible for the drafting of imperial edicts. Many people went on to higher posts from Hanlinyuan.

Since the Southern Song Dynasty (1127-1279), the contents of the exam papers, the questions, the topics, etc., were officially restricted to the Four Books variorum by the Confucian scholar Zhu Xi (1130-1200). The four books were the *Great Learning*, the *Doctrine of the Mean*, the *Analects of Confucius* and *Mencius*, all of which were considered Confucian classics. The topic for the examination would be based on the Four Books, and in answering the questions, the examinees were required to develop their idea in accordance with Zhu Xi's annotation, i.e. achieve glory by writing on behalf of the sage. The examinees were not allowed to put out their ideas as they pleased. As for the stylistics, the eight-part essay was adopted in the examination at the provincial and capital levels. The eight-part essay, with each part having specific content, asked for a composition of 450-600 words. The palace examination asked the examinees to write a *Celun*, that is, a political essay.

The above-mentioned examination was held for civilian posts. The examination for the selection of military officers was called *Wuju*. Except for the content of the examination, the two examinations had a lot in common—the procedures, the titles for the successful candidates, and the posts set.

The imperial examination system, with its many advantages and its just as many disadvantages, came to its prime in the Ming and Qing dynasties. As the major means of the selection of officials, the system fired people's enthusiasm to learn and brought about a major advancement in culture and education; at the same time, thanks to the system, people set too much emphasis on reading books and looked down upon other social professions. As a popular slogan of that time went: all trades were of the lowest grade, except for reading. Many people did more than 10 years of hard study in constrained circumstances for the sake of becoming famous overnight or holding a government post. A lot of people began taking examinations at an early age for the sake of official honor and were still doing so in vain when they grew old, only to let their youth slip idly by. If they succeeded, of course, they went into raptures. During the Qing Dynasty, a satirical novel called *The Scholars* was released, specially written to denounce feudal scholars and the imperial examination. In the novel, the main character, Fan Jin, distinguishes himself in the examination after years of failed attempts. However, he is so excited upon hearing the news that he goes mad shortly after, before he can benefit from his success. The story of Fan Jin profoundly reflected the effects of the imperial examination on people. The content of the examination was strictly stipulated, which imposed restrictions on people's free thinking and invalidated their wisdom and creativeness. The eight-part essay became no more than wordplay, which had nothing to do with either the national economy or people's livelihood. No wonder some people attributed the destruction of the Ming Dynasty to the eight-part essay.

In the palace examination, examinees were asked to write an essay on current affairs, which would be presented to the emperor as advice on government policy; but in the Qing Dynasty the handwriting of the examinee was regarded as more important, so the examinations in fact turned out to be a calligraphy contest. Seeing the number of government posts, the enrollment quota was strictly limited. Only 200-odd people survived the national examination, which was to say, of the countless competitors only a small fraction were successful. Indeed, the imperial examination system did pick out excellent people, but only at the expense of unnecessary waste and tremendous sacrifice. It was because of the fierce competition that the practice of fraud in the examinations worsened.

The civil service examination of the Western world gained so many lessons from the imperial examination system of China that some Westerners referred to it as the Fifth Great Invention of China. At the end of the Ming Dynasty and the beginning of the Qing Dynasty (16th-17th century), European missionaries arrived in China in succession, and the Chinese imperial examination system aroused their interest and curiosity. They showed great appreciation for the system, and introduced it in Europe, matching *Xiucai, Juren*, and *Jinshi* with Bachelor, Master and Doctor respectively. Detailed and accurate descriptions of the imperial examinations of China were given in *Matteo Ricci's Notes About China*. During the European Enlightenment of the 18th century, a lot of French and English thinkers had admiration and esteem for the fair-minded and impartial examination system. Voltaire was profuse in praise; even Montesquieu, who was critical about China, showed appreciation of the Chinese imperial examination and utilized it as an example to attack the practice of selling official posts and titles, which was in vogue for a time in France. France first enforced the civil service examination during the revolution in 1791, and Germany and England followed suit in 1800 and 1855 respectively. It was generally held that the European civil service examination used the principles and concrete measures of the Chinese imperial examination for reference. The examination system for civil servants officially practiced in China today is an inheritance from the historic imperial examination.

Although the imperial examination system made its own positive contributions to history, it was out of touch with the times, especially after the Western countries invaded China in the middle of the 19th century. In the face of flourishing global capitalism, the system no longer suited present needs. One of the main historical themes of modern China was modernization. The imperial examination did not include any knowledge of science, technology, history and geography of the world, international law, management, etc., which were essential for modernization. Obviously, the system had become a stumbling block in the way of advancing China.

Under such circumstances, men of vision appealed for reforming the imperial examination system; others advocated abolishing it altogether. In 1905, the government of the Qing Dynasty declared the system null and void.

3. Literature and Art

During its long history, the Chinese nation produced manifold and magnificent literary arts, which are now not only the jewels of the nation, but an inalienable part of the treasure-house of world literature.

Literature

In the pre-Qin period, Chinese literature appeared in the form of poetry, debate, prose, etc. Afterwards, every dynasty contributed to the development of literature in its own way.

Shijing, or the *Book of Songs*, was the first general collection of Chinese poems. It included 305 poems with a time span of over 500 years, from the early Western Zhou Dynasty (1100-771 BC) to the middle of the Spring and Autumn Period (770-476 BC). In the collection, there were orations of royal sacrificial rites and folk songs which circulated widely among people, reflecting the political and social lives of people of that time. Some of its chapters were widely beloved and read for a time, such as its first chapter *Guanju* (an osprey), which depicted a young lad who missed his girl and conceived a happy married life in mind. The first four lines read:

Merrily the ospreys cry,

On the islet in the stream.

Gentle and graceful is the girl,

A fit wife for the gentleman.

These poems were often lyricized and turned into songs, but the music scores were lost later on. Thus, the *Book of Songs* that we see today is in fact a collection of words of songs, and we can still sense the beauty of their rhyme and rhythm.

In the late Warring States Period (475-221 BC), a new pattern of poetry, *Chuci* (the *Poetry of Chu*), was born in the State of Chu in south China, which had jurisdiction over today's Hubei and Hunan provinces. What characterized *Chuci* was rich imagination, a splendid romantic style, diversity of words, a grandiose and lengthy structure, as well as its frequent application of modal words like " 兮 (*xi*)", " 些 (*xie*)", etc. An outstanding writer of

Qu Yuan

Chuci was Qu Yuan (340-278 BC), the first great poet in the history of China. Qu Yuan held a senior position in government, which entitled him to participate in making both domestic and foreign policies. However, he was framed and sent into exile later on. During his exile, he wrote a large number of poems to express his depression and heavy heart, showing a deep concern for state affairs. In the end, when the king refused to listen to his advice, Qu Yuan jumped in a river and took his life. Legend holds that when the locals learnt the news, they immediately went to save him in their boats. They threw rice balls into the river to distract the fish and shrimps away from his body. Since then, in memory of Qu Yuan, people hold dragon boat races every year and eat *zongzi*, a pyramid-shaped dumpling made of glutinous rice wrapped in bamboo or reed leaves. A major traditional festival, the Dragon Boat Festival, came into being.

During the Han Dynasty (206 BC-AD 220), a form of rhymed prose evolved from *Chuci—fu*. *Fu*, a kind of noble royal court literature, had even more of a grandiose structure and exquisite diction. The major representative composer of *fu* was Sima Xiangru (179-117 BC). Sima was once depressed over his lack of success. One day, he was a guest of a wealthy family, and after learning that the rich and powerful host had a beautiful girl named Zhuo Wenjun, he showed his love to her by playing love songs on the Chinese zither. Zhuo Wenjun had long admired his talent, so she eloped with him. Though he was a man

The annual Dragon Boat Festival commemorates Qu Yuan.

of learning, Sima was penniless and frustrated. In order to support their family, they opened a public house, selling liquor, and the wife served behind the counter. When the news reached her father, he could do nothing but send them money and servants, despite still feeling angry. Not long after, Sima was favored with opportunities to compose *Shanglin Fu* and several other pieces for the emperor; the emperor loved his work and put him in an important position at last.

There was yet another great work to come out of the Han Dynasty—*Records of the Historian* by Sima Qian (145-90 BC). On one hand, the book was first and foremost a historical work, recording the history of China from remote antiquity to the author's time, and creating the style of presenting history in a series of biographies. From then on, every dynasty followed the tradition set by Sima in compiling the history of the previous dynasty, thus leaving an unbroken record of the history of China—*Twenty-Four Histories*. On the other hand, the book was regarded as a literary work. His description of the historical events and figures was so succinct in style and vivid in image that even the famous writer

Sima Qian

and thinker of modern China, Lu Xun (1881-1936), praised it as "a historical masterpiece and an unrhymed epic through the ages".

In the Wei and Jin periods (220-420) and the Southern and Northern Dynasties (420-581), poetry developed further and went through a transition from the five-character verse to the eight-line poem, each containing five or seven characters with a strict tonal pattern and rhyme scheme. Cao Cao (155-220) was an excellent statesman, a strategist and a poet. His poems, solemn and stirring, vehement and fervent for the most part, reflected his boldness of vision and pioneered a new style. In his poem *Though the Tortoise is Old*, for example, he laments the rapid changes occurring in the world: life is short and no one can ever escape one's doom, even the great men and the heroes. However, we also read another implication in the same lines: so long as one has breath left, one should never stop fighting for a righteous cause.

An old steed, though confined to the stable,

His mind was on the road thousands of miles away.

A man of ambition retains his high aspirations even in old age,

The heart of an ageing hero is as stout as ever.

His lines expressed his lofty sentiments beautifully, and have been appreciated by innumerable intellectuals for many many years.

In contrast to Cao Cao, a later poet, Tao Yuanming, pursued a quiet and comfortable life. His poems sang praises of the joys of idyllic life. In *Back Living in the Pastoral and Drinking*, he wrote:

My house is built amid the world of men,

Yet little sound and fury do I ken.

I tell you how on earth I can dip blind, any place is calm for a

peaceful mind.

I pluck hedge-side chrysanthemums with pleasure,

And see the tranquil Southern Mount in leisure.

The evening haze enshrouds it in fine weather, while flocks of

birds are flying home together.

The view provides some veritable truth, but my defining words

seem to me uncouth.

Because his poems struck one as natural, pure, refreshing and lofty-minded, he was rightly called a Pastoral Poet.

In the Southern and Northern Dynasties, a lengthy narrative poem, *The Ballard of Mulan*, was produced among the people in the north of China. The story: a young girl, Mulan, disguises herself as a man to substitute her father for army duty, and after

Hulao Pass from the *Romance of the Three Kingdoms*, New Year painting, Qing Dynasty

Mulan Joining the Army, New Year painting by Yang Liuqing, Qing Dynasty

performing outstanding feats in the war, she rejects the official posts conferred on her and returns home to be reunited with her family. The plain lines portray her mentality exquisitely. Mulan, an artistic character was thus loved deeply by Chinese people and was known all over China, and the story is still adapted to theatre, film and many other art forms.

In the Tang Dynasty (618-907), poetry reached its peak. About 50,000 poems by 2,300 authors were handed down to our time, well-preserved. The era had an astonishing diversity of authors— emperors, aristocrats, bureaucrats, men of letters, as well as monks, nuns, Taoist priests, prostitutes, etc., and it was safe to say that poetry was the most popular literary form. At the time, emperors highly esteemed poetry and attached great importance to poems in the imperial examination. It was said that Zu Yong only distinguished himself in these exams at capital level with his poem on the assigned subject, *Looking at the Zhongnan Mountain After Snowfall*. His poem reads:

How lovely is this northern slope of Zhongnan!

Piled with fresh snow, above the clouds it leaps;

The sun emerging, the trees regain their color,

But to the city a colder evening creeps.

In less than 20 words, the writer depicted not only the snowy mountainous scenery of Zhongnan, but also set off the leitmotiv of the poem by contrasting the scenery and people's impressions. This is the best representation of poetry that is simple in language but rich in meaning.

The poems of the Tang Dynasty had strict restrictions on rhymes, and were particular about the number of lines, words and tonal patterns. Li Bai, Du Fu, and Bai Juyi were three of the most prominent writers in the history of Tang. Li Bai, eulogized as the Celestial of Poet, was adept in depicting magnificent natural grace. His poems were rich in fantastic visions, artistic exaggerations and romantic boldness. His poem *The Waterfall on Mount Lu Viewed from Below* went:

The sunlit Censer Peak exhales incense-like cloud,

Like an upended stream the cataract sounds loud.

Its torrent dashes down three thousand feet from high,

As if the Milk Way fell from the blue sky.

Gazing at the Waterfalls of Mount Lushan, from a poem by Li Bai, painted by Xie Shichen, Ming Dynasty

Du Fu was lauded as the Sage Poet. His poems, for the most part, were a mirror of the social life of the time, especially that of the weal and woe of the people. In a way, his works were treated as authentic records of history. *Around the vermilion gates the reek of meat and wine /over the street where lie the bones of the frozen dead*—well-known lines about the polarization of wealth. Bai Juyi's poems were characterized by their simplicity, and were easy to understand. It was said that the poet would read his poem to illiterate grannies after he finished writing one; if they didn't understand, he would amend it until the poem got through to them. From a poem he wrote at 16:

Wild grasses spreading over the plain

With every season come and go.

Heath fire can't burn them up, again

They rise when the vernal winds blow.

Their fragrance overruns the pathway;

Their color invades the ruined town.

Seeing my friend going away,

My sorrow grows like grass overgrown.

It was said that one day, he paid a formal visit to a well-known poet with his poem, but the poet made fun of him when he saw his name first, saying: "Rice is expensive in Chang'an (the capital of the Tang Dynasty, present-day Xi'an) and it's not easy to live here."

But when he moved on to the line, *Heath fire can't burn them up*, he could not help praising him: "If you can make such good poems, there will be no difficulty in living here any more."

The Tang Dynasty witnessed the highest achievement in Chinese poetry. Some of the more famous lines are still widely read, after over 1,000 years. Today many pre-school children, before they learn to read, begin to recite poems of the Tang Dynasty under the guidance of their parents or grandparents. Any Chinese person, as long as he has received education of some sort, can recite a few poems of the Tang Dynasty from memory.

By the Song Dynasty (960-1279), *Ci* took over as the main literary form. *Ci* comprised lyrics that were adapted to a pre-composed tune. Unlike poems that asked for a sameness in the number of characters of every line, *Ci* varied in the length of the lines. Owing to the variation in length, *Ci* was also referred to as "long-and-short verse", some in one stanza, and others in two stanzas. Compared to poems of the Tang Dynasty, *Ci* featured more complicated ideas and bigger structures. Among the famous composers of *Ci* are Liu Yong (958-1503), Su Shi (1036-1101) and Li Qingzhao (1084-1151). The *Ci* of Liu Yong's impressed one as graceful and restrained, while that of Su Shi's was bold and unconstrained.

It was said that once Su Shi asked a minstrel how he would compare his songs with those of Liu Yong's.

The minstrel replied: "Liu Yong's songs are only suitable for young girls of 17 or 18 who beat time gently with ivory crescent-moon clappers, singing in a soft voice: *Moored by a riverbank planted with willow trees/ beneath the waning moon and in the morning breeze*; as for your songs, I think they must be sung by hefty fellows who beat time hard with iron clappers, singing loudly and heartily the words of your song: *The great river eastward flows/ With its waves are gone all those/ Gallant heroes of bygone years*."

Su Shi loved the analogy, which he thought appropriately distinguished the two styles. Li Qingzhao was a well-known female purveyor of Song Dynasty *Ci*. Her works were full of feminine sentimentality, especially after she tasted to the full the bitter-ness of a wandering life: drifting from place to place, homeless and miserable, because of the war; and to make things worse, her husband died, which made her poems sound even more plaintive and mournful. For example, her poem *Slow, Slow, Tune* began with seven pairs of reiterative locutions, which affected every reader of them with a gloomy mood:

I look for what I miss

I know not what it is.

I feel so sad, so drear,

So lonely, without cheer.

Yuan Qu was a type of verse popular in the Yuan Dynasty (1206-1368), and included *Zaju* and *Sanqu*. *Zaju*, poetic drama or proto-drama, was comprehensive art, including singing, dancing, spoken parts, acrobatic fighting, etc. *Zaju*, each telling a complete story, consisted of four acts or four scenes, with one character having the singing role (the main role) in each scene. Besides, there was *Xiezi* in *Zaju*, which was equal to prologue. The important playwrights of the Yuan Dynasty were Guan Hanqing (1225-1300) and Wang Shifu (whose dates of birth and death are unknown, but whose main literary creations took place between 1295 and 1307). The representative work of Guan Hanqing was *The Injustice Done to Dou E* (also known as *Snow in Midsummer*). Dou E, a young and pretty widow, lives with her mother-in-law. One day, her mother-in-law meets with danger, and it happens that the hooligan Donkey Zhang and his father pass by and help her mother-in-law. Next, they take advantage of the opportunity and propose to Dou E and her mother-in-law, but are rejected. Donkey Zhang plots to poison her mother-in-law so as to compel Dou E to submit. But his father takes the poison by accident. So he frames a case against Dou E for poisoning his father, and Dou E is sentenced to death. To plead her innocence, Dou E makes three big wishes on the execution ground: that her blood will splatter on white silk, that it will snow in June and there will be a drought lasting for three years. In the end, all her wishes come true. And three years later, her soul brings a lawsuit through a newly appointed official and

Pottery figurines in the form of a poetic drama of the Yuan Dynasty

the wrong is righted.

The representative work of Wang Shifu was *Romance of the Western Chamber*, which told a complicated love story between the prime minister's daughter, Cui Yingying, and a young intellectual, Zhang Hong. In graceful and refined language, the writer meticulously depicted the mentality of young people in love, extolling Cui Yingying for smashing the bonds of feudal ethics in brave pursuit of love. The first time the play was put on the stage, it brought the house down, drawing applause especially from the scores of young people in the audience. The best of the writer's intentions: "May all the lovers get their due love," has become a permanent theme of many literary works. The stories of *Dou E* and *Romance of the Western Chamber* are widely available in various artistic forms even today.

Sanqu was a type of verse, with tonal patterns modeled on tunes drawn from folk music. Each *sanqu* had a *gongdiao* and

Romance of the Western Chamber, written by Wang Shifu, Yuan Dynasty

a *qupai*. *Gongdiao* was mode of music, marking the rising and falling tones of syllables; *qupai*, the name of the tune, sets rules for the number of the words and verses, the rhymes and the tonal patterns of a song. Compared with *Ci*, the length of *sanqu* was even more flexible. The sentence could be as short as one word or as long as 20 or 30 words. The representative writer of *sanqu* was Ma Zhiyuan. The following is an excerpt from an oft-quoted and widely loved poem by him, *Tune to "Sand and Sky"—Autumn Thoughts*:

> *Dry vine, old tree, crows at dusk;*
> *Low bridge, running stream, cottages;*
> *Ancient road, west wind, lean nag.*
> *The sun setting west,*
> *And one with breaking heart at the sky's edge.*

In the poem, the author piled eleven images one upon another, and in depicting a bleak and dreary late autumn evening, he threw into sharp relief the loneliness and gloomy mood of a man leaving his native land and family and wandering in a strange land.

The novels of the Ming (1368-1644) and Qing (1644-1911) dynasties were renowned. In fact, novels originated much earlier, but in the form of short stories, and their plots were relatively simple. Novels developed fully in the Ming and Qing Dynasties, and the four famous ones were *Romance of Three Kingdoms, Outlaws of the Marsh, Journey to the West* and *A Dream of Red Mansions*, which were jointly called the Four Classics of China.

The *Romance of Three Kingdoms* was created by Luo Guanzhong between the end of the Ming Dynasty and the beginning of the Qing Dynasty, narrating the intricate political and military struggle of the Three Kingdoms period. In the book, Zhuge Liang was the most successfully portrayed character, who, wise, faithful and full of stratagems, was regarded as the embodiment of the wisdom and loyalty of the Chinese people. *Outlaws of the Marsh* was written by Shi Nai'an on the basis of folk legend at the end of the Yuan Dynasty and beginning of the Ming Dynasty. The book was improved upon by different writers, and after the last revision by Jin Shengtan at the end of Ming, it became set. The story, analogous to that of Robin Hood of England, told that in the last years of the Northern Song Dynasty (960-1127) a group of hero-brigands were forced to become sworn brothers and sisters, rise in rebellion against the oppression of the government and root out thugs to reassure the people.

Wu Cheng'en of the Ming Dynasty produced *Journey to the West* according to the related stories of proto-drama of the Yuan Dynasty and prompt-books used by storytellers. The book tells about the deeds of Xuan Zang of the Tang Dynasty, on a pilgrimage to India for Buddhist scriptures. With the aid of his three capable and talented disciples, the Monkey King, Pigsy, and Monk Sha, he

A Dream of Red Mansions, written by Cao Xueqin, Qing Dynasty

defeats monsters of every size and description, overcomes natural obstacles of all forms, and finally arrives at the Western Heaven and gets the authentic Buddhist scriptures. The novel was a model for Chinese mythological novels.

The author of *A Dream of Red Mansions* was Cao Xueqin (1715-1764). The common thread that runs through the book is the love story between Jia Baoyu and Lin Daiyu. By depicting the rise and decline of an aristocratic family, the book unfolded all the aspects of social life of the Qing Dynasty, covering philosophy, history, literature, calligraphy, painting and

drawing, religion, medicine and divination, eating and drinking, clothing and customs and so on. It was therefore called the encyclopedia of traditional culture of China. All the above-mentioned novels had dramatic and intricate plots, vivid scenes, lifelike images, concise and expressive characters. It was as if, while reading them, people were participating, and they could hear and see with their own eyes. Doubtlessly, these books are of great artistic value.

It is thus clear that Chinese literature was abundant in literary forms and styles, rich in content and subject, and enormous in numbers. Many of these beautiful poems and stories are on everyone's lips even today, and enjoy great popularity in western countries.

Art

The ancient art of China was colorful and magnificent. What follows is a brief introduction of ancient calligraphy, drawing and painting, architecture and horticulture, which typically reflect the uniqueness of Chinese art and their undying charm lasting to this day.

Calligraphy

Calligraphy is the art of hand-writing of characters. It calls for a combination of the writer's aesthetic taste and his personality. It is one of the art forms that bears the most distinctive Chinese characteristics.

The Chinese characters are ideography that has developed from pictography. The characters were constructed on the basis of six strokes: the horizontal stroke, the vertical stroke, the left-falling stroke, the right-falling stroke (which starts with a stroke ' \ ', then slants downward to the lower right corner and ends with a slight bend), dot, and the hook stroke (at the end of a horizontal or vertical stroke to form the shape of a hook). Different combinations of strokes form different characters.

Before the Tang Dynasty (618-907), the characteristic of calligraphy lay in the evolution of the writing styles. The earliest mature characters known in China were *Buci*, inscriptions engraved on bones or tortoise shells, which had broken away from primitive scribbles and laid a foundation for the basic forms of Chinese characters. After the first emperor of the Qin Dynasty (221-206 BC) unified China, he gradually standardized the writing styles of the characters. The product of this standardization was *Xiaozhuan*, namely, the lesser seal character, which was slender in shape and uniform in thickness. The lines of the lesser seal character were roundish, as if embracing one another, and a page of characters were like a crisscross network, neat, tidy, in good order, and appealing to the eyes. In the Han Dynasty (206 BC-AD 220), *Lishu*, the official script, became the major writing form. The characters turned square-and-squat-shaped. The strokes were various in thickness and the lines switched over to squaring with abrupt pausing, bending, turning, etc., looking at once plain and simple, daring and energetic. The simplification and rapidity of the official script led to the cursive script. The cursive script, lively, vivid and unstrained, best gave expression to the writer's fervor and best displayed his individual character.

In the Three Kingdoms period (220-280), the regular script, also known as orthodox writing or authentic writing, developed from the official script. The regular script looked neat and tidy, square and upright, so calligraphy learners of later generations took the regular script as the point of departure. In the Jin Dynasty (265-420) the running script was all the rage. The running script, a writing form between the regular script and the cursive script,

Oracle-bone inscriptions

Preface to the Orchid Pavilion, by Wang Xizhi

gave the impression of being leisurely and sincere, graceful and natural. The most famous calligrapher of that time was Wang Xizhi, the Sage of Calligraphy, whose renowned representative work, *Preface to the Orchid Pavilion*, was generally acknowledged as the "number one running script under the sky". The Tang Dynasty brought calligraphy to an age of great prosperity, especially the regular script, for people in the Tang thought highly of maintaining standards, and they thought only by some established standard or norm could one tell the inferior and the bad from the superior and the good. The regular script best embodied the norm of calligraphy.

Tang, a dynasty for calligraphers, saw a large number of them come forth. Of the Four Great Calligraphers, three lived in Tang: they were Ouyang Xun (557-641), Yan Zhenqing (709-785), and Liu Gongquan (778-865). The other one, Zhao Mengyao (1254-1322), lived in the Yuan Dynasty (1279-1368). Although they all used the regular script, each of them possessed a characteristic of his own: the Ouyang style was characterized by vigorous brushstrokes and compact structures; the Yan style incorporated suggestions of the seal characters in the regular script, and was marked by well-shaped, magnificent brushstrokes and the full-bodied solidity and statuesque grace of the characters; the Liu style had forceful and thinner strokes. Yan Zhenqing and Liu Gongquan enjoyed equal fame, and their calligraphy was summed up as "Yan's vein (meaning 'integrity') and Liu's bone ('strength')". By now all the forms of Chinese calligraphy were defined.

From the middle of the Tang Dynasty, the development of Chinese calligraphy entered a period of variations of styles. From Song Dynasty, calligraphy became the monopoly of the intellectuals and there appeared a so-called calligraphy of men of letters.

The handwriting did not follow a standard any more, but sought to convey the writer's own emotion, interest and charms, demonstrating an intense artistic personality. During this period there was an emperor calligrapher, Emperor Huizong of the Song Dynasty, Zhao Ji (1082-1135). He did not attend to his proper duties as an emperor, but created a handwriting style, "Lean Gold Style", which was characterized by its thin, hard, incisive strokes and distinctive turns and bends in characters. On the basis of the regular script, the cursive script, the official script, the seal script and the running script, the calligraphers constantly brought forth new ideas, blazed new trails, gave free rein to their creativeness and talent, and finally made art blossom in radiant splendor. Chinese calligraphy exerted such a tremendous and lasting influence on Japan and the Korean Peninsula that calligraphy flourishes in these countries even today.

To be good at calligraphy, unremitting efforts were a must. There are many Chinese anecdotes about how hard people worked at calligraphy. It is said that Wang Xizhi, the Sage of Calligraphy, kept on practicing all the time, and even when he was walking, he did not stop practicing. He so frequently wrote and scribbled with his fingers on his clothes as he walked, that he poked holes in them. His son, Wang Xianzhi, loved calligraphy too and wrote beautifully at an early age. He was determined to be a great calligrapher like his father, but his mother told him that he could only realize his lofty aspiration after he had used up 18 jars of water in practicing. Another five years of hard work passed, and Wang Xianzhi thought that good enough. So he presented what he wrote, a " 大 ", to his father. Though his father was fairly pleased with his progress, he picked up a brush and added a dot under the character. Afterwards, when Wang Xianzhi showed his work to his mother, she pointed at the dot added by Wang Xizhi, and heaved a sigh, saying: "Only the dot looks like what your father writes."

Wang Xianzhi was embarrassed, but he went on practicing and worked even harder at calligraphy. He finally realized his dream and became a famous calligrapher like his father. The descendant of Wang Xizhi in the 7th generation, Monk Zhiyong, was an ardent fan of calligraphy too. It was said that he kept practicing every day, and the worn-out brushes alone filled ten big baskets. Predictably, he became a famous calligrapher too. Legend holds that people poured into his temple, and visited him to get his handwriting sample or make him write on a signboard. Not long after, the threshold of the temple was wrecked, and had to be wrapped in iron sheets.

There is one more thing left for clarification: the main tools of calligraphy are the writing brush, China ink, paper, and ink-stone. In a sense, it is the flawless collocation of them—the four treasures of the study—that formed the extremely subtle art of calligraphy.

The Art of Painting and Drawing

Drawing and painting in China had an early start. Painting on silk emerged as early as in the Warring States Period (475-221 BC). In the Han Dynasty (206 BC-AD 220), apart from paintings on silk, people did frescos on the walls of caves and stone, brick relief on ancient Chinese tombs and shrines. According to reliable historical records, there appeared several famous artists since the Three Kingdoms period (220-280).

Gu Kaizhi (346-407) of the Eastern Jin Dynasty (317-420), a popular artist for a period of time, put forward a new theory of painting and drawing, which had profound and far-reaching influences on the development of Chinese art. The painting and drawing of this period featured figure painting and animal painting. The Sui and Tang dynasties saw a big advancement in ancient Chinese art and a large number of artists came to the fore: Zhan Ziqian

(550-604) of the Sui Dynasty (581-618),
Yan Liben (?-673) and Wu Daozi (685-758)
of the Tang Dynasty (618-907), etc.
Though the paintings still featured people,
the two of the three main subject matters
of traditional Chinese art—flower-and-
bird painting, landscape painting—were
in the making. Zhan Ziqian was skilled
in landscape painting. His picture, *A
Spring Outing*, a treasure handed down
from generation to generation, unfolded a
magnificent scene of rivers and mountains,
and visitors who lingered in the scene
and were reluctant to leave. It was as if
a one-foot-long scroll encompassed a
thousand kilometers of magnificent land-

scapes: the blue mountains, green trees, clear waters, fresh flowers
and all kinds of visitors—it was a representative of the early
Chinese works of landscape.

Portrait of Liu Xiu,
Emperor Guangwu
of the Han Dynasty,
painted by Yan Liben,
Tang Dynasty

Yan Liben was an expert in portraying people's mien. His
famous work *Sedan Chair* conjured up the grand spectacle of
Emperor Taizong of the Tang Dynasty receiving the Tibetan envoy
Lu Dongzan, who was sent by the Tibetan King Songtsam Gambo
(*c.* 617-650) on a diplomatic mission to meet the Tang princess
Wencheng. It was of great historical significance. Wu Daozi,
reputed as the Sage of Painting, was skilled at mountains, waters,
flowers, trees, and animals. He was good at figure painting too,
especially the legendary Buddhist and Taoist people. His masterpiece was *The King of Heaven Seeing Off His Son*. The picture
depicted a story that went like this: after the birth of Sakyamuni,
the founder of Buddhism, his parents carried him in their arms to

pay religious homage to the holy temple and deities. The ribbons on the clothes of Wu's characters looked as if they were fluttering in wind. From then on, he was revered as the forefather of the trade of painting by the craftsmen engaged in it.

The art of fresco hit its prime during the Sui and Tang dynasties. The subject matters of fresco were comprehensive, and covering people, Buddhist and Taoist anecdotes, mountains and waters, flowers and bamboos, birds and beasts, etc. The lines of the fresco were either forcefully compact and well-knit or carefully drawn and precise; either leisurely and liberal, or lofty and high spirited. The colors were gorgeous and splendid. All in all, the fresco of Sui and Tang showed a high artistic level.

The art of ancient Chinese painting reached another peak in the Song Dynasty. At the time, people regarded calligraphy and painting as elegant mental activities and cultural accomplishments. They created a clear-cut aesthetic norm for painting. The content, the forms, and the skills of the art took on a new aspect of all-round development. A distinctive system began to take shape in both artistic practice and theory. Emperor Huizong of the Song Dynasty, Zhao Ji, was not only a famous calligrapher, but a famous all-round artist, who did well in painting flowers and birds.

The landscape painting was in full bloom in the Yuan Dynasty (1279-1368), constituting the artistic mainstream. Painting featuring withered trees, bamboos and rocks, plums and orchids, etc., achieved remarkable success. Loaded with the artist's moral integrity and view of the world, these subject matters signified being noble and unsullied, proud and aloof. The idea guiding the artistic creation of the Yuan Dynasty could be summarized as the advocacy of neglecting appearance and concentrating on likeness in spirit, holding the ancient people's suggestion in high esteem and devoting much attention to the expression of the writer's subjective interest and enthusiasm. In practicing, the artists were particular about natural charm; skills in ink and wash became the main technique; pictures were much valued for being plain and simple instead of being excessively florid and richly ornamented—all of which heralded the combination of the ink-and-wash, the flower-and-bird and the freehand-brushwork painting. The Yuan pictures strove for the integration of poem, calligraphy and painting. One man worthy of mention here is Zhao Mengfu. As both calligrapher and artist, he advocated that calligraphy and painting had the same origin, and that the strokes of calligraphy should be suitable for painting. He upheld the belief of modeling oneself after nature, claiming "cloudy mountains everywhere were my teachers." His theory and practice had great impact on the later ages.

In the Ming and Qing dynasties, the ancient Chinese art of painting and drawing reached great heights. The painting of this period was characterized by a change of painting styles and swarms of schools of painting. With respect to subject matter, figure painting, landscape painting, Chinese flower-and-bird painting, as well as other miscellaneous pictures embodying the emotional appeal of the intellectual, took precedence. Many schools of art came into being, some boasting special painting styles, some differentiated from others by location. In other words, the Chinese painting in this period witnessed a large number of new artists, each expressing his or her artistic view in a different way, like so many colorful flowers blossoming in the garden of art.

Ancient Chinese art of painting differed widely from classical Western painting in many aspects:

First, the tools. Chinese artists used brushes, ink, watercolors, silk, and paper. The brush was soft, and after it was put to paper, nothing could be changed. In Western painting, the common tools were oils, canvas, and oil pens. The oil pen was hard, allowing repeated alterations when necessary.

Second, the technique. Chinese artists laid stress on lines, paying scant attention to color or perspective or foreground or background, while Western artists did the opposite.

Third, artistic conception. Chinese artists racked their brains in the pursuit of an artistic conception to reflect their values, and their love and hate, in the picture. They gave little consideration to whether the subject was accurately presented. The painting was more a symbolic and expressive tool than a reproduction of the subject. Western artists were demanding in their accuracy. As a camera takes pictures, so an artist did his job. They regarded the reappearance of the subject and its lifelikeness as more important.

Lastly, the subject matter. Chinese paintings revealed the natural scene more, especially in landscape paintings, where people were purposely made small and insignificant, to show the concept of "harmony of man with nature". The Western paintings featured human beings, and even in their landscape paintings, people occupied prominent positions in the composition. Their paintings were a reflection of the exploration of nature and the conquest of nature by men.

The difference between Chinese and Western paintings lay, in fact, in the difference between the two ways of thinking, two cultures and two traditions.

Architecture and Horticulture

Buildings are not only utilitarian but artistic as well. In the course of history, a lot of systematic architecture came and went, but three managed to survive until today: Chinese architecture, Islamic architecture and European architecture.

Chinese architecture was the product of evolution over a massively long period of history. In the Han Dynasty (206 BC-AD

220), buildings of timber and brick gradually matured into things of beauty. Afterwards, with the enhancement of the technique of constructing the wooden structures and the quality of brick and tile, the Song government standardized the units of the building, such as a beam, a column, etc. A special document of that time, *The Standardized Techniques in Construction*, summarized the experiences accumulated so far. By the Ming and Qing dynasties, both the building materials and skills peaked in terms of quality. Bricks and tiles were in common use, and the official buildings were highly standardized and patterned. In 1723, the Qing government announced *Regulations of the Construction Engineering by the Ministry of Works*, to unify the standardization in building material and the modulus of the official buildings.

The ancient Chinese buildings had many unique characteristics. With respect to building material, they were different from European buildings, which were constructed mainly with stone and rock, and were largely made of timber, bamboo, brick and tile. As early as in the Han Dynasty, buildings of timber and brick structure came into being and evolved. Afterwards, even finer timber was discovered, and the skills involved in processing the timber were constantly upgraded. Many buildings of the timber structure avoided using any binder or adhesive or nails. Solely by fitting a tenon into a mortise to make a joint and thus hold two pieces of timber together, a tall building could be erected. The skill levels involved in baking brick and tile escalated: the brick was more and more close-textured, enduring, strong, resplendent and artistic. The advantage of a building made of timber and brick was clear to see—a short period of construction. The huge Forbidden City of Beijing was built in a mere 10 odd years. However, the defects of these buildings were no less evident: they were prone to ageing and decay. On the contrary, the buildings made of stone and rock

A bird's-eye view of the Forbidden City

lasted much longer, some as long as hundreds of years; the Notre Dame Cathedral, for instance, has lasted 182 years.

Ancient Chinese builders thought highly of architectural aesthetics, which generally took the shape of a group of well-arranged courtyards. No matter what it was, an imperial palace or an official building, a residence of a wealthy family or a temple, a typical Chinese building was always made up of several independent houses and courtyards, enclosed with verandas, walls, etc. Even the residence of an average family had some flank rooms, though not very many, to collocate with the main building. Except for the garden, a Chinese building usually took on a layout of axial symmetry: the primary buildings in the longitudinal axis and the secondary buildings on both sides symmetrically. Different independent buildings functioned differently: those in the front were sitting-rooms, meeting-rooms or offices, and were open to the outside; those at the back were living rooms and bedrooms, an area belonging to womenfolk of a family, and were not open to the outside. The Forbidden City and quadrangles in the north of China typically embodied the principle of the architectural complex. The overall arrangement had a charm of its own, that is, you had to go into one courtyard in order to go into another, and every courtyard greeted you with a different view, unlike European buildings, which, seen from the outside, could be clearly taken in at a glance.

Ancient Chinese buildings had respect for colored drawings on buildings, which served many functions. First, the painting pigment protected the building from damp, wind erosion, and insects. Second, it served as a symbol of the social position and status of the owners. For example, the use of colors was subject to restriction: in the Ming and Qing dynasties, red and yellow were stipulated as the most honorable and the noblest colors, which could only be used on royal buildings. Of course, they also

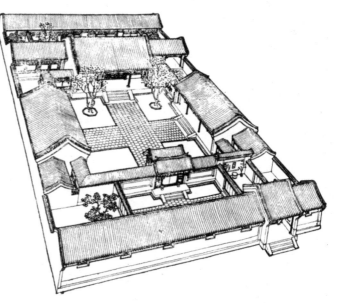

Traditional Chinese quadrangle houses

functioned as ornaments for a building. Colored drawings as decoration most often appeared on the beams of inner and outer roofs, corbel brackets, ceilings, sunk panels and column caps of houses. The composition closely matched the shape of the structure. The painting, elaborate in drawing and rich in color, made an intense visual impression on people, bringing them sensory satisfaction. Colored drawings were abundant in patterns and subject matter, which included people, mountains and waters, flowers, feathers, Chinese characters like " 福 " (happiness) and " 寿 " (longevity). The dragon and phoenix were royal prerogatives, not allowed for ordinary people.

Horticulture had a close tie with architecture. As early as in the Shang Dynasty (c.1600-1100 BC), the Chinese people started making use of natural mountains, lakes, rivers and springs, trees and flowers, birds and animals, to build gardens. The purpose of building a garden was to let the grasses and trees, birds and animals, multiply undisturbed in a conservation area. In some gardens or parks, pavilions were built and pools dug for the conve-

The Summer Resort, a masterpiece of Chinese landscape architecture, painted by Leng Mei, Qing Dynasty.

nience of the emperor and his nobility, for the purpose of entertainment and hunting. After Qin Shi Huang unified China, he invested all the financial and intellectual resources of the nation into the building of the Shanglinyuan Garden, an imperial garden. He built pools and the legendary island in it in the hope of creating a fairyland.

In the Wei and Jin periods and the Southern and Northern Dynasties, the style of gardening switched over to naturalism, and rich and powerful people began building their private gardens. Conforming to the level of literary art, horticulture ripened in the Tang and Song dynasties. Poems and painting were blended with the layout of the garden and the making of scenery; the skills required in piling stones, rock-filling, and water-arrangement, were widely applied to building a garden. In the Ming and Qing dynasties, gardening entered a phase that approached perfection. No matter what it was applied to, a royal garden or a noble's private garden, the art reached its summit in design and construction. Most of the superbly preserved gardens in China today are heritages of the Ming and Qing dynasties, such as the imperial Summer Palace and Beihai Park in Beijing, and the private Zhuozheng Garden and Wangshi Garden in Suzhou. They all typically represent the uniqueness and high skills in landscaping.

Unlike European gardening, which took geometric design as its main expressive form and had obvious artificial vestiges, Chinese gardening is after the natural charm of mountains and rivers, etc. Generally speaking, a Chinese garden consisted of rockeries, waters, vegetables and buildings, and, occasionally, animals. All the elemental components were required to be in accordance with nature, represent nature and avoid artificial vestiges as much as possible. Every rockery, every miniature river, every flower and every tree must be carefully arranged to tally with natural laws: water meandering, flowing, and falling, sometimes like a river, sometimes like a waterfall; in piling up a rockery, so much attention was focused on the texture of stone that it complied with that of a natural one; the trees and flowers were artistically and naturally spaced.

The buildings in the garden were of great variety and artistic value. Except for the corridors and verandas and bridges, the others

Zhuozheng Garden

were generally called pavilions and towers. Of them, some were built for taking a rest, some for sight-seeing, some for the gathering of friends. All in all, people spared nothing in drawing near nature. They appreciated natural delights, relaxed both mind and body in nature, molded their temperaments and cultivated their moral characters in it. Chinese gardening embodied the traditional concept of "harmony of man with nature", and comforming to the nature.

Chapter 8

Communication with Foreign Countries

China is situated on the eastern part of the Eurasian continent. It borders the sea in the east, and the high mountain ridges on its western and southwestern border separate it from West Asia and Southwest Asia. In ancient times, numerous mountains and rivers kept it apart from Europe, leaving only comparatively convenient land transportation to several countries in its northeast and southeast. However, this relative geographical occlusion did not make the Chinese people isolated. During the country's long-term historical development, the Chinese people ventured out courageously again and again, maintaining close contacts not only with neighboring countries but also directly or indirectly with distant European and African countries. In this intercourse between China and foreign countries, the Chinese civilization spread outward and at the same time, China also assimilated many foreign civilizations, making its own cultural and material life immensely richer.

1. The Silk Road

Most people know that the Silk Road was an ancient trade route across the Eurasian Continent, and silk, of course, was the most important product along the route. In the late 19th century, the German geographer, Ferdinand von Richthofen, christened this channel the Silk Road. Subsequently, scholars called the oceanic transport route connecting the East and the West the Maritime Silk Road.

In ancient times, the ancestors of the Chinese nation were already expert at sericulture and silk fabric production. In 1955, archeologists discovered various fabrics such as silk patches, silk ribbons and silk threads—dating back to 4,700 years ago—in southeast China's Zhejiang Province. Amongst Shang oracle-bone inscriptions dating back to more than 4,000 years ago, there exist characters for "silkworm", "silk" and so on. According to them, silk fabrics have a history of about 5,000 years in China. Since the Spring and Autumn Period, silk fabrics, together with bamboo slips, had become the main writing materials.

As early as the pre-Qin period, silk had begun to spread to the West. According to legend, King Mu (976-922 BC) of the Zhou Dynasty (1100-256 BC) loved traveling to faraway places. After going west through the Kunlun Mountains, he reached the court of the so-called Queen Mother of the West. Among the gifts that he presented to the Queen

Mulberries and sericulture

Mother of the West were white *gui* (an elongated pointed tablet of jade held in the hands of ancient rulers on ceremonial occasions), black *bi* (a round flat piece of jade with a hole in its center) and plenty of colored silk fabrics. *The Biography of King Mu*, a book from the Warring States Period (475-221 BC), recorded this. If true, silk must have started traveling west as early as 1000 BC. Research by scholars has shown that King Mu of the Zhou Dynasty traveled west along the Yellow River to Gansu via Ningxia, then passed across Qinghai and went through the Kunlun Mountains into Xinjiang. Crossing Congling (the Pamirs), he reached the Iranian plateau of Central Asia, where perhaps the Queen Mother of the West used to be. When he returned, he chose to go through Ili Valley. Passing the northern foothills of Tianshan Mountain, he came back to Central Shaanxi, the capital of the Zhou Dynasty. Whether or not King Mu actually presented the Queen Mother of the West with silk fabrics, his travels undoubtedly laid a foundation for the opening of the Silk Road. After that, China had intermittent

Yumen Pass

exchanges with Central Asia, their alliance hanging precariously by a thread, as it were. We could say that the Silk Road came into being gradually through the common role played by the states and nations fringing it, during their economic and trade exchanges.

As a symbol of the existence of the Silk Road, Zhang Qian of the Han Dynasty (206 BC-AD 220) went to the Western Regions as an envoy. The Western Regions was a generic term for the areas to the west of the Yumen Pass and Yang Pass (located respectively to the northwest and southwest of present-day Dunhuang, Gansu Province).

During the Qin (221-206 BC) and Han dynasties, the Hun nomads living in the northern Mongolian Plateau kept traveling further south and launching predatory wars on the relatively affluent inland areas. The Qin and Han rulers thus began to build the Great Wall to resist their aggression on one hand, and on the other, adopted a pro-Hun policy to appease the Huns with plenty of silk, jewelry, gold and silver. By the early years of the Western Han Dynasty (206 BC-AD 25), the Huns had expanded their territory into the Western Regions. When Emperor Wu (who reigned from 140 BC to AD 87), an emperor of rare gifts and bold strategies, ascended the throne, the Han Dynasty had already reached its peak. In order to remove the Hun threat, he sent Zhang Qian to the Western Regions as an envoy, in an attempt to forge an alliance with Darouzhi (Dairujing), a minority that had been an enemy of the Huns, to make a pincer attack on the Huns.

Zhang Qian, born in Chenggu County, Shaanxi Province, was an imperial guard. In 139 BC, over a hundred people led by Zhang Qian set out for the Western Regions for the first time. To reach the Western Regions, they had to go through areas controlled by the Huns. Cautious as Zhang Qian and his entourage were, the Huns captured them in Hexi Corridor (now the northwest of Gansu).

Zhang Qian's Mission to the Western Regions, early Tang Dynasty mural painting. Mounted, right, is Han Emperor Wu, with Zhang Qian kneeling before him.

They detained them in the royal court of the Huns (now near Huhhot, Inner Mongolia). Employing coercion and inducement, they compelled him to marry a Hun woman, who bore him several children. Zhang Qian stayed in Hun for 10 years. In the meantime, under oppression by the Huns and its ally Wu Sun, the Darouzhi people continued to migrate westward and settled in the Weishui region near the Aral Sea.

But Zhang Qian never forgot his original mission. One day in 129 BC, he left his wife and children; leading his entourage, he fled from the royal court of the Huns. Using abilities he had learnt from the Huns during the decade, he escaped from the Hun-controlled zone and went on westward. Crossing the vast Gobi Desert in raging sandstorms and surmounting the snowfield of Congling (the Pamirs) in the bitter cold, they reached Darouzhi at last. Unexpectedly, since Darouzhi now had abundant products in their new homeland, their people lived a comfortable life, and did not intend to take revenge on the Huns at any cost. Zhang Qian stayed there for more than a year but failed to convince the Darouzhi people to enter into an alliance with the Han Dynasty and launch a pincer attack against the Huns.

On their way home, in order to avoid the Huns, they changed their route. After re-crossing Congling (the Pamirs), they converted their route from the original Northern Route along the northern part of the Tarim Basin to the Southern Route in the south of it. They entered the Qiang-controlled zone by way of Qinghai, only to find that the Qiang people had now become vassals to the Huns. The Huns captured Zhang Qian and his entourage again. More than a year later, Zhang Qian, with his Hun wife and the remaining entourage, fled back to Chang'an in 126 BC.

Zhang Qian paid a heavy price for this diplomatic mission. It took him 13 years at the expense of hundreds of people, and he did not even complete the mission. However, the journey helped extend the political and cultural forces of the Dynasty in the Central Plains to the vast regions west of Yumen Pass and Yang Pass. It not only helped strengthen contact between the present-day Xinjiang region and inland areas, but also that between China and Central Asia, West Asia and South Asia as well; second, his trip threw light on the geographical situation of the age—each state's location, products, population, cities and towns, military strength, etc. This was important for the Han government to set relevant policies. In addition, Sima Qian preserved these records in *Records of the Historian*, and later on, they became valuable information for the study of the ancient geography and history of those regions and states.

Afterwards, Han continued to launch large-scale operations against the Huns. In 119 BC, Emperor Wu sent his generals Wei Qing and Huo Qubing to command a massive punitive expedition northward; together they defeated the main Hun forces. The vanguard of the Han army reached today's Lake Baikal directly. By now, the whole of the Hexi Corridor had come under the control of the Han Dynasty, which had set up administrative agencies there. There was no sign of the Huns to the south of the desert. However, Emperor Wu was afraid that the Huns were likely to use some of their subsidiary states in the Western Regions to wait for an opportunity to strike back. In order to uproot the threaten from the Huns, in the same year, he sent Zhang Qian once more as an envoy to the Western Regions to contact Wusun. This time, Zhang Qian led a 300-member mission, with more than ten thousand heads of cattle and sheep, plenty of gold, coins and silk. They went all the way west with great strength and vigor. When they arrived in the State of Wusun, Zhang Qian conducted negotiations with Wusun; in the meantime he sent his vice-envoys to visit the States of Dawan (the Fergana Basin lying on the western foothills of the Pamirs), Kangju (between Lake Balkhash and the Aral Sea in the south of present-day Kazakhstan), Darouzhi (lying in the upper reaches of the Amu-Dar'ya on the western foothills of the Pamirs), Daxia (lying between the Hindu Kush and the upper reaches of the Amu Dar'ya), Anxi (Iran and Iraq today) and Shendu (India today). They established diplomatic relations with these states, further expanding the influence of Han Dynasty to the regions west of Congling.

Zhang Qian's second mission to the Western Regions enhanced the Han power over the areas east and west of Congling and those over the north and south of the Tianshan Mountains. In 60 BC, the Han government established in Luntai, Xinjiang, the Western Regions Area Command, wielding jurisdiction over the vast areas south of Lake Balkhash and east and west of Congling. They then opened up communication between China and the West. Along the passage opened up by Zhang Qian on his mission, groups of envoys and traveling merchants between China and various states of the Western Regions made frequent exchanges in an endless stream. There were at least more than one hundred people in each batch. Among the goods exported from China, silk not only accounted for the largest quantity but it was the most famous and precious as well. This was the reason why Ferdinand von Richthofen came up with the name Silk Road.

Zhang Qian's missions to the West integrated the areas north and south of the Tianshan Mountains with the Central Plains for the first time. They strengthened the political, economic and cultural exchanges between the Han Dynasty and the Western Regions, and played an important role in the formation and development of a unified multinational country. The world-famous Silk Road opened up, a vital communication line to West Asia by way of China's Xinjiang region, promoting economic and cultural exchanges between China and various countries in Asia, Europe, and Africa. Zhang Qian, now renowned as a great pioneer, would forever be remembered in the pages of history. His contributions towards the opening up of the Silk Road inspired generations of Chinese people.

During Wang Mang's reign (9-23), the various states in the Western Regions were once again under the control of the Huns, and the Silk Road was cut off. The Eastern Han (25-220) government sent a punitive expedition against the Huns, and in the meantime sent Ban Chao to various states in the Western Regions as an envoy to unify the states to fight against the Huns. Finally they expelled the Hun forces. During this time, Ban Chao sent his subordinate, Gan Ying, to Daqin (the Roman Empire) as an envoy. Gan Ying traveled to the Persian Gulf, but upon hearing that the sea before him was too vast to cross, he returned. This was the most distant place the Han officials had traveled westward along the Silk

Road. Ban Chao then re-opened the Silk Road.

The starting point of the Silk Road was China's capital at the time, Chang'an (now Xi'an). It extended westwards through the Hexi Corridor and bifurcated into the northern and southern routes: the northern route extended northwest through the Yumen Pass and went west along the southern foot of the Tianshan Mountains and the northern rim of the Tarim Basin. It crossed Congling in present-day Kashi and went west through the Fergana Basin and Samarkand (now Uzbekistan); the southern route extended southwest out of Yang Pass, and went west along the northern foot of the Kunlun Mountains and southern rim of the Tarim Basin. Passing by Shache, crossing Congling, it went west by way of the upper and middle reaches of the now Amu Dar'ya. The two routes above met in Mali, which lay in now Turkmenistan, and then went west to the eastern coast of the Mediterranean Sea via present-day Damghan, Hamadan (both in the north of Iran) and Baghdad (present-day capital of Iraq) southeast of the Caspian Sea. Here it bifurcated and turned to Europe and Africa separately. The above was the main route of the Silk Road, which also had a branch line that went from now Afghanistan southward to India.

Other Sino-foreign trade routes were inspired by the Silk Road. One was the Maritime Silk Road. It set out from the following ports along China's coast: Fanyu (later called Guangzhou), Dengzhou (now Yantai), Yangzhou, Mingzhou (now Ningbo), Quanzhou and Liujiagang; then it extended east to Korea and Japan, and afterwards went south to various countries in Southeast Asia and turned west to Arab and coastal countries in East Africa. It began in the Qin and Han dynasties, prospered during the Sui and Tang dynasties, flourished further in the Song and Yuan dynasties, peaked in the early Ming Dynasty, and declined in the middle of Ming Dynasty due to a ban on maritime trade. As people transported and sold well-known ceramics from China and spices from the West by way of this maritime line of communication, they called it the Road of Ceramics or the Road of Spices and Ceramics.

The other was the Southern Silk Road. It extended from Sichuan to India, wandering through high mountain ridges. It was opened up in approximately 4 BC; however, people from the Central Plains did not know about it. When Zhang Qian went on his mission to the Western Regions, he found Sichuan cloth in the State of Daxia and Qionglai bamboo walking sticks produced in the Sichuan region. Knowing that someone had bought them from others in Shendu, he reported the case to Emperor Wu of Han, who ordered him to take charge of the situation. He had the passage explored. The route started from Chengdu, entering Myanmar by way of Yunnan, then making a detour to India. The Southern Silk Road lasted for more than two thousand years. During the War of Resistance Against Japanese Aggression, the Japanese cut off the passage to the sea in the grand hinterland, and the transport of goods on the Yunnan-Burma Road, and China-India Road opened up along the Southern Silk Road was extremely busy and became the lifeline of logistic support for the hinterland.

But the Silk Road was the main channel of business for most people. China's silk, porcelain, etc. were transported to all parts of the world, while grapes, alfalfa, walnuts, sesame seed, pepper, pomegranates, etc., not to mention fine-bred horses, were introduced to China. In addition, there were technological and cultural exchanges as well. For example, China's irrigation technology (qanats) and sericulture technology spread to foreign shores, while foreign arts like *huqin* (a two-stringed bowed instrument) playing, acrobatics, magic, dances and so on became an integral part of traditional Chinese culture.

The opening up of the Silk Road was a major chapter in the history of human civilization. The various ethnic groups along the route worked together and created it, so it was a road of friendship and a road of cooperation as well. It greatly facilitated East-West economic, cultural, religious, and linguistic exchanges. In addition, it promoted the progress of science and technology, cultural communication, and political exchanges between various ethnic groups; it introduced a new phase in the development of human civilization.

2. The Eastern Sailings of Jianzhen and Western Voyages of Zheng He

Jianzhen (687-763) was a Vinaya (a sect) Buddhist monk in Tang Dynasty. He was born in Yangzhou, Jiangsu Province and his secular name was Chun Yu. At that time, his country was under the reign of Wu Zetian (624-705, the only female emperor in China's history). Buddhism was flourishing and in fashion for a time. Influenced by the spirit of the time, Jianzhen became

Monk Jianzhen

a monk at the age of 14, and later made study tours to Luoyang and Chang'an. He apprenticed himself to many celebrated monks and read extensively; however, he did not rigidly adhere to the views of his own sect. He not only conducted a systematic study of Buddhism, but also mastered architecture, sculpture, medicine, calligraphy and so on, becoming a monk of multifaceted cultural accomplishments.

In 715, he returned to Yangzhou to practice Buddhism in Daming Temple. He took charge of the temple in 733 and became a local Buddhist leader. People said that he had as many as forty thousand disciples, which won him the reputation of "the sole Buddhist master in the areas between the Yangtze River and the Huaihe River".

Jianzhen lived in the golden age of the Tang Dynasty (618-907), which attracted many foreigners for business, sight-seeing, and learning. Most of them came from Japan. Japan sent so-called "Kentoshi Envoys to Tang" to China on many occasions, and along with them came students and monks, eager to learn about the advanced civilization of China. Besides, the envoys and monks from Japan also took the opportunity to find suitable Chinese monks and invite them to promulgate "real" Buddhism in Japan.

Among the tenth batch of the envoys were Japanese student monks Rongrui and Puzhao, who had heard of Jianzhen and came to Yangzhou in 742, urging him to sail east to Japan to disseminate Buddhist doctrines. They said, "Buddhism has spread east to Japan, where there are now temples and monks, but there's no one who can promulgate the doctrines and initiate people into Buddhism. There was a Shōtoku Taishi in our country before, and he had predicted that a holy religion would thrive in Japan in 200 years' time. Now 200 years have passed and we hope that you can travel east and make the religion prosper."

Jianzhen replied to them, "I have heard that Zen master Huisi of the previous Nan Yue kingdom passed away after his relocation and was reborn as the prince of ancient Japan. He made Buddhism flourish and saved humanity from a sea of misery. I also heard that Japan's Nagaya-no-ōkimi worshiped Buddhism, and made a thousand *kasayas* as alms for monks and other people of great virtue. The edges of his *kasayas* were embroidered with four sentences: 'We live near different mountains and rivers; but we share the winds and the moon under the same sky; we place hope on all of us Buddhists; we lay the basis for our future relationship.'

It seems that Buddhism is predestined to thrive in Japan."

Jianzhen asked his disciples whether any of them would like to go to Japan as a teacher, but none of them spoke. After a long time, an apprentice named Xiangyan replied, "That country is too far away, so it will be hard to stay alive. The sea between our lands is so vast that no one out of a hundred will reach the other side. We have not practiced Buddhism well and our thorough transformation has not happened yet. This is why the monks are silent."

At this, Jianzhen was furious and said, "We are going there to spread Buddhism, how can we care about our lives? Since you are not willing to go, I will go by myself!" Thereafter, one by one, his disciples agreed to accompany him.

Crossing the sea east to Japan was far from smooth sailing, exactly as the Chinese saying goes, "The road to happiness is strewn with setbacks." In the winter of 742, Jianzhen and his disciples, along with some Japanese monks, set about building ships, preparing for their journey east. One day, a disciple named Daohang jokingly taunted another named Ruhai, saying the latter had not mastered the Buddhist doctrines and so should not go to Japan. Ruhai took it seriously and became very angry. Then he falsely accused Jianzhen and his men of building ships in an attempt to collude with pirates, in order to attack Yangzhou. The local authorities promptly arrested Jianzhen and his men. Though they quickly ascertained the truth, Jainzhen's first attempt to sail east was aborted.

In January 744, after careful preparations, Jianzhen made his second attempt, with more than 100 disciples, artisans, etc. in tow. But hardly had they set off when the powerful waves within the Yangtze River estuary gripped their ship and damaged it. It took them a month to repair the ship.

On their third attempt, they met with high winds. After

drifting to the Zhoushan Islands, they were rescued and taken to the Asoka Temple in Yuyao (now Ningbo, Zhejiang Province). For a while after that, monks in various parts of Zhejiang invited Jianzhen to teach Buddhist doctrines and disciplines. In order to retain him, a monk reported to the local authorities that monk Rongrui from Japan would entice monk Jianzhen to go to Japan. Therefore, the local authorities arrested Rongrui, who later escaped only by pretending to die of illness.

After leaving the Asoka Temple, Jianzhen led his men south. They had intended to buy a ship in Fujian to sail east, but the authorities at Wenzhou stopped them. As it turned out, the disciples at Daming Temple worried about the safety of their master, and pleaded with the Yangzhou authorities to deliver an official document to Zhejiang authorities, asking them to stop Jianzhen. His fourth attempt thus came up short again.

In 748, Jianzhen made his fifth attempt. On the East China Sea, they encountered a strong northerly wind, which blew them southward all the way. After more than 10 days of drifting, they found themselves ashore at Zhenzhou (present-day Sanya, Hainan Province). Jianzhen stayed in Hainan for a year and brought there lots of cultural and medical knowledge from the Central Plains. Today, such relics of Jianzhen's East Sailing as "scripture-drying slope" and "big and small Buddhist caves" can still be found there. Later, passing through Guilin, Guangzhou, etc, Jianzhen taught Buddhist scriptures and doctrines. During this time, Rongrui, who had actively persuaded him to go to Japan, died of illness and Puzhao took his leave. Moreover, Jianzhen had acclimatized poorly, and been exhausted from his trip, then he became blind in both eyes as a result of inappropriate treatment. Nevertheless, his determination did not waver at all and he vowed to go to Japan to promote Buddhism.

In 753, Japanese envoys Fujiwara Kiyokawa, Kibi no Makibi and Abe-no Nakamaro (Chinese name Chao Heng) made a special trip to Yangzhou, urging Jianzhen to sail east together with them. Chao Heng had studied in China for years and even taken up a government post. On November 16, Jianzhen and his party boarded the ship of Japanese envoy, and set sail from the Yangtze River estuary for Japan. In his company this time were 14 disciples, as well as laymen, 24 people in all. The items they carried included various Buddha statues, bodhisattva statues, Buddhist sariras (scrolls of Buddhist scriptures, precepts books, Fan Chuang (long narrow flags on which there were Buddhist scriptures), various gold and jade utensils, ornaments, and copybooks by Wang Xizhi, Wang Xianzhi and other famous calligraphers. On December 20, Jianzhen and his party arrived in Kushikino, Kagoshima, and finally set foot on Japanese soil.

Jianzhen received a warm welcome from the Japanese government and numerous monks. In February the next year, Jianzhen was received into the Todaiji Temple of Nara, capital city of Japan. The King of Japan sent his gifts and best wishes through a royal edict, conferring on him the title of Dharma-Spreading Master, and

Japanese monks welcome Jianzhen

declaring, "From now on, the monk is given free rein to conduct initiation and teach doctrines." Also, together with another eminent local monk of the Huayan sect, Jianzhen would be in charge of Buddhist affairs in Japan. In April, Jianzhen erected an altar in Todaiji Temple,

The Yangzhou Daming Temple where Monk Jianzhen practiced self-cultivation

preaching Buddhist precepts to about 500 people, including the emperor, the empress, the crown prince and other royal members and monks. Moreover, he built three Altar Temples in succession and established a formal system of commandments. Jianzhen thus became revered as the founder of the Japanese Vinaya.

In 759, Jianzhen's disciples completed works on Toshodai Temple, and Jianzhen moved there. The emperor ordered that Japanese monks had to study in Toshodai Temple before their initiation into monkhood; thus Toshodai Temple became Japan's highest institution of Buddhism. On May 6, 763, Jianzhen passed away in the temple, which has now become one of Japan's national treasures.

Jianzhen not only took dharma to Japan, but also promoted Chinese culture there, and this had a far-reaching impact on Japan with respect to Buddhism, medicine, calligraphy and so on. It could be said that Jianzhen was an outstanding Chinese cultural envoy to Japan. This was precisely why he enjoyed a high reputation both in China and Japan, and was commemorated by the peoples of both countries. In 1963, on the 1200th anniversary of Jianzhen's death,

Statue of Zheng He, Jinning County, Kunming, Yunnan Province

Buddhist communities in both China and Japan held large-scale celebrations, and the Japanese Buddhist community named the year "The Year Master Jianzhen's Evidence Appeared." In 1980, through the mediation of Deng Xiaoping, Moriki Kyoujunn, the abbot of Toshodai Temple, accompanied the dry-lacquer statue of Jianzhen to Yangzhou, Jianzhen's hometown, to "visit relatives". Daming Temple was thus rebuilt. This became a major event in the history of Sino-Japanese diplomatic relations.

Zheng He's western voyages were feats that evoked not only pride in the Chinese, but also pity.

Zheng He, originally named Ma Sanbao, was born into a Muslim family in Kunyang (present-day Jinning County, Kunming City), Yunnan Province, in 1371. His ancestors came from Central Asia, and his grandfather and great-grandfather had made pilgrimages to Mecca. Their exotic experiences, the way they had braved the wind and waves all the way to Mecca, aroused great curiosity in Zheng He at an early age.

When he was 11 years old, the newly established Ming government dispatched its great troops to Yunnan in order to accomplish the great cause of reunification of the country. The war brought about the Ming government's unification of Yunnan, and it changed Zheng He's fate as well. During the war, Zheng was captured by the Ming army. The rules of the Ming Dynasty stated that child prisoners would have to be castrated, and so Zheng He had to undergo the torturous procedure. After that, Zheng He fought for the Ming army in one place after another; difficult living conditions tempered his will while the vagaries of war cultivated his talent. At the age of 19, Zhu Di, the then King of Yan, later the third emperor of the Ming Dynasty, chose him as a personal bodyguard. During the four-year fight for the throne, he followed Zhu Di to different places, risking his life, achieving one exploit after another, and becoming one of the major heroes to help Zhu Di seize power and mount the throne. He was then granted the family name Zheng by Zhu Di and changed his name from Ma Sanbao to Zheng He. Known as Emperor Yongle, Zhu Di placed his trust squarely on Zheng He and promoted him to the rank of Supervisor of Imperial Eunuchs, the highest rank among Imperial Eunuchs.

In 1405, the third year after Zhu Di had ascended the throne, he decided to send Zheng He as an envoy to the Western Seas. The then Western Seas referred to the seas west of South China Sea (west of 110 degrees east longitude) and the coastal areas around, which extended to the Indian Peninsula, coastal areas around the

Part of Zheng He's nautical charts for his western voyages

Persian Gulf and the Red Sea, and Northeast Africa. One of Zhu Di's motives in dispatching Zheng He to the Western Seas was to find Emperor Jianwen, who had been overthrown by him and was said to have escaped overseas. However, a more important mission for Zheng He was to establish diplomatic relations with various countries, and to promote the prestige of the great Ming Empire and Chinese civilization.

Since Zheng He did not have the distractions of family and fatherhood, he could concentrate on his career ideals. History had offered him the chance to realize his dreams.

On July 11, 1405, leading a huge fleet comprising more than 240 ships and 27,800 people, Zheng He set out on his first voyage. During the next 30 years, he made six such voyages as a leader of his fleet. According to historical records, he visited more than 30 countries and regions, reached the farthest east coast of Africa, and was likely to have been to Australia. The places include: Java, Sumatra, Sulu archipelago, the Philippines, the Malay Peninsula, Siam (Thailand today), Cambodia, Kozhikode, west coast of India, Aden, Mecca, Hormuz, and Mogadishu, Somalia and so on. In 2002, Gavin Menzies, a British naval officer, published a book entitled *1421, The Year China Discovered the World* (London: Bantam Press, 2002). He believed that Zheng He's fleet not only reached the Western Seas, but had been to the Americas, Australia and the Arctic region, and was the first global navigation. However, people have generally not recognized his assumptions.

At the time, China had mastered advanced shipbuilding technology. There

Zheng He's Western Voyages, Ming Dynasty woodblock print

were five types of ships in his fleet, with treasure ships dominating. There were also horse ships, grain ships, living ships and war ships, among which the largest, the treasure ship, was more than 138 meters long and 56 meters wide. The ship had four decks, wore 12 sails, and could hold a thousand people. Moreover, each of the fleets bound for the Western Seas was massive in scale. Four of these voyages are clearly mentioned in histor- ical records, and each carried

Pavilion in Zheng He's hometown, inside which stands a stele in his honor.

over 27,000 people. You can imagine what a spectacular sight it was as the fleet cut through the oceans mightily.

China had also mastered advanced navigation technology. The ancient Chinese had learned to determine the position by observing the sun, moon, and stars. By the end of the Northern Song Dynasty, they began to use compass in navigation. By combining astronom- ical positioning and navigation with a compass, Zheng He's fleet could accurately determine the vessels' position and course.

Zheng He was not only an eminent leader and navigator, but also a diplomat with strategic insight. As they came ashore on Java, on their first journey to the Western Seas, the Javanese, not knowing these were Chinese, killed more than 170 crewmembers. Zheng He's soldiers were furious, and were ready to attack the Javanese. Though Zheng He was also livid, he restrained his men, knowing that the purpose of sailing to the Western Seas was not only to show off a powerful China, but also to establish friendly relations with various countries. If they attacked the Javanese, it would cause suspicion and panic in other countries. After learning about the fact, the king of Java immediately sent someone to settle it.

Zheng He's trips were journeys of peace. Although his fleet possessed overwhelming military power, it was just for self-defense, and never took the initiative to attack others. In spite of the fact that China was already a powerful country at the time, he was cordial with every nation, treating them equally without discrimination. Zheng He's sincerity won him a warm welcome everywhere he went. Many nations sent emissaries to China to pay tribute, some countries' kings leading the way. According to statistics, during Zhu Di's reign of 22 years, envoys from Asian and African countries, where Zheng He had visited, visited China 318 times, with an annual average of over 14 times. A maximum of 18 countries sent their emissaries to China simultaneously. In addition, three of the kings passed away during their visit to China, and unexpectedly, asked before their deaths that they should be buried in China. The Ming government gave them all grand burials befitting princes. Zheng He's magnificent feat helped the propagation of Chinese civilization and the introduction of foreign cultures, writing a new chapter in the history of cultural exchanges between China and foreign countries.

In 1431, Zheng He set out on his seventh and final voyage. He was 60 years old, and was realizing his long-cherished dream of making a pilgrimage to Mecca. However, perennial exposure to winds and waves and the heavy workload took their toll on him. Two years later, on his voyage home, he died of illness.

Zheng He's western voyages were not only unprecedented

in China, but also unparalleled in the world at the time. His first journey preceded Christopher Columbus' discovery of the "New Continent" by 87 years, and Vasco da Gama's navigation around the Cape of Good Hope to the Indian coast by 93 years. It preceded Magellan's global navigation by more than 110 years. Besides, his first voyage was much bigger in scale. Columbus' largest fleet only comprised 17 ships and a crew of about 1,200 to 1,500 people; Vasco da Gama's largest had 20 ships and a crew of about 170 people; Magellan only had five ships and a crew of 265 people.

It is a pity that the Ming government put a halt to its maritime activities after Zheng's voyages; hence, China was no longer a maritime superpower. In sharp contrast, Western countries were eager to sail the globe, and decades later, there appeared the geographical discovery that changed the world. If China had continued its maritime activities, what would the result have been? What would have happened if Zheng He's massive fleet had encountered Columbus's, Vasco da Gama's or Magellan's? It is a pity that history cannot afford imagination.

Of course, Zheng He deserved to be commemorated by the Chinese people. In 1987, the Chinese People's Liberation Army Navy named one of its training ships *Zheng He*. Since July 11, 2005—the anniversary of Zheng He's maiden voyage—the day has been designated as China's Maritime Festival. Zheng He's tomb and memorial in Nanjing receive an endless stream of people who come to pay tribute to him. The dauntless, enterprising spirit of Zheng He, as well as his broad vision of peaceful and friendly coexistence with various countries, is a valuable spiritual legacy for the Chinese nation.

3. Marco Polo and the Missionaries

Marco Polo

Due to widespread dissemination of *The Travels of Marco Polo*, his name was not unfamiliar to the Chinese. As for the question of whether Marco Polo had really been to China, many western scholars hold either a doubting or completely negative attitude. Some even think that someone may have used Marco Polo's name to create false records. The records in *The Travels of Marco Polo*, according to them, contain many elements that are inconsistent with facts and seem vaunting. The Chinese commonly believe that Marco Polo did come to China, and according to the account of *The Travels of Marco Polo*, his story is generally as follows:

Marco Polo was a Venetian, and Venice was a city celebrated for its prosperous trade and commerce. Marco Polo's father and uncle were both merchants, and lived during the Yuan Dynasty era in China. Marco Polo's father was Niccolo Polo, and his uncle, Maffeo Polo. The Polo brothers went east in 1253, looking for business prospects. Around 1265, they ran into a diplomatic mission from Mongolia in Central Asia and followed it to China. The reigning emperor was Kublai Khan, an emperor of great talent and bold vision, who extended hospitality to guests from afar.

Christianity had already spread to China, and the people of the Yuan Dynasty called it the "Yelikewen Religion". Kublai Khan had acquainted himself well with Christianity. So, taking this opportunity, he appointed the Polo brothers as his special envoys, and sent them back to Europe to pay a visit to the Pope. He hoped the Pope would dispatch 100 clergymen to China for missionary work. Because of the hardships of the journey, the Polo brothers took more than three years to return to Europe, only to hear that the Pope had passed away, and the new Pope had not yet been elected. They had no choice but to go back home and wait.

Now it was nearly 16 years since they had departed from Venice. Already 15 years old, Marco Polo saw his father and uncle for the first time. Their experiences excited him, and their descriptions of China fascinated him. Subsequently, when the Polo brothers presented themselves before the new Pope and returned to China, the 17-year-old Marco Polo accompanied them. The new Pope also dispatched two clergymen to go to China with them.

It was a hard journey from Europe to China, and occasionally dangerous. They had to traverse rough roads, pass through tribal battlefields, with bandits and robbers coming and going from time to time. Before they reached halfway, the two clergymen returned to Europe, because of the hardships and dangers of the journey. Originally, the group had planned to go to Hormuz from where they would go to China by sea, but the remaining members did not find a ship at the time due to local wars. Therefore, they could not but turn their steps eastward. Trudging across the desolate and bloodcurdling Iranian desert, over the rugged and chill Pamirs, they entered China.

In *The Travels of Marco Polo*, there are detailed accounts of their hardships. Once a group of bandits surrounded them, and only after battling fiercely and hacking to death a few of the bandits did they dash out of the siege. During the attack, Marco Polo and his father were wounded as well. Before long he had developed a high fever. What was worse, they did not have any water left. Under such circumstances, they had to continue to move forward until they found some water. Finally, shored up with water and a rest, they moved on again. Only when they had reached Bada Mountain did they get a good rest. Crossing the Hindu Kush, they were caught in a snowstorm and even faced a snowslide, but were luckily rescued by some Lamas. While traversing the vast desert (present-day Xinjiang region) they had to struggle with water shortages and intense heat. After a hard trek of three-and-a-half years, in the summer of 1275 they eventually arrived in Shangdu (situated in today's Plain Blue Banner of Inner Mongolia), the summer capital of the Mongol Empire. Marco Polo was 21.

They received a warm welcome from Kublai Khan. When summer had passed, they went with Kublai Khan to Dadu, capital of the Yuan Empire (present-day Beijing City). The Mongolians called it Hanbali. Marco Polo's powers of observation and attention to detail, coupled with a good memory, enabled him to satisfactorily answer Kublai Khan's questions about his journey to China. Khan sent him to south China to investigate the situation on agricultural production and industry and commerce. Leading the entourage Khan had appointed for him, Marco Polo went in succession to Yangzhou, Zhenjiang, Suzhou, Hangzhou, Fuzhou, Xiamen and so on, returning to Beijing by ship by way of the Grand Canal. In the meantime, he sent back many reports, summing up the situation in respect of products, resources, revenues, folkways, etc. of the places he had been to. This gladdened Kublai Khan, who then dispatched him to Yangzhou to take charge of local revenues. Afterward, Khan sent him once more as an envoy to some countries in Southeast Asia, including Burma, India, and Ceylon.

Every aspect of China was strange to Marco Polo: large expanses of land, rich resources, a large population, prosperous industry and commerce; magnificent palaces, roads leading to all parts of the country and post houses used for document delivery, paper currency, coal, water timers, kites that could fly and deliver messages, convenient type printing, and the beautiful marble bridge south of Beijing City (Lugou Bridge, still called Marco Polo

Bridge by Westerners)…all these were so novel and magical to him and left such a deep impression on him, that he seemed intoxicated when he recollected them later.

Marco Polo's father and uncle had stayed in China for a long time, so they missed their hometown and family members. They begged Kublai Khan to let them go home, but he turned down their requests several times. In 1292, a vassal Mongolian king who ruled Persia sent a messenger to Kublai Khan with the news that his queen had died, and he hoped he could choose a new queen from her family. Kublai Khan agreed. The Polo family saw it as a good opportunity, and asked Khan to let them escort the queen to Persia, so that they could also go home and visit their relatives. Kublai Khan granted their requests and gave them substantial rewards. The Polo family had stayed in China for 17 years; Marco Polo was 38 years old, and his father and uncle were old. After sending the new queen to her destination, they took a few days' rest and then set out for home. In 1295, they returned to the hometown that they had left 24 years previously.

The huge wealth the Polo family brought back home, and their stories about the Orient caused a sensation in their hometown. Young Marco Polo was often chased around by people who wanted to listen to his stories. He generously repeated what he knew. As he often used seemingly exaggerated terms such as "several million" to describe China—for example, "Emperor Kublai possesses millions of precious stones"—people nicknamed him "Mr. Million".

Three years later, a fierce war broke out between Venice and Genoa. To defend the interests of Venice, Marco Polo entered the war. In the end, Venice lost the war and Marco Polo was captured and put into prison in Genoa. In prison, to satisfy people's curiosity as well as to pass time, he patiently related his stories. Among the listeners, there was an observant and conscientious man called

Rustichello, who found Marco Polo's stories very interesting. After obtaining his consent, the man recorded them in French, the most popular language at the time. These records became the famous *The Travels of Marco Polo*. In 1299, after his release from prison, the great explorer got married, and later had three daughters. In 1324, Marco Polo passed away.

The Travels of Marco Polo is the first travelogue written by an European to contain a detailed depiction of China. Its appearance aroused widespread interest, and people soon translated it into other European languages and it quickly spread all over. Christopher Columbus, the great 15th-century navigator, read *The Travels of Marco Polo* in detail, and annotated it. He yearned very much for the affluence of the Orient described in the book, and made up his mind to go to the East in search of wealth. From 1492 onwards, funded by the King of Spain, he made three long voyages. In the belief that he had reached the East, he arrived in the Americas, thus discovering a "New Continent" serendipitously. *The Travels of Marco Polo* is now stored in Lisbon, the capital of Portugal, with the many annotations and commentaries made by Columbus when he was reading it.

However, as the account narrated by Marco Polo was too strange, or too fantastic, many people suspected that he had never been to China. They did not believe that there were such countries in the Orient as described by him, and that China was affluent, powerful and highly civilized. As the story went, Marco Polo's relatives and friends also suspected that he had told a monstrous lie. Perturbed at this, in his dying days, they asked him to repent to God and confess that he had fabricated *The Travels*. But Marco Polo refused, and declared that not only had he not lied and exaggerated, but had not told of even half of the strange happenings that had occurred on his travels.

According to statistics, up until now, *The Travels of Marco Polo* has had about 119 versions. Scholars generally believe that the book is no ordinary travel notes. For China, it had great historical value, whereas for Europeans, it broadened their horizons, spreading out before them a strange and massive world. Maurice Collis, a scholar who studies Marco Polo in the West, believes that *The Travels of Marco Polo* was "not a simple travel note, but an enlightened work. For ignorant Europeans, it was the same as awakening the deaf. It demonstrated a brand new field of knowledge and vision before the Europeans. The significance of this book is that it led to extensive rejuvenations of the European Human Sciences." (Maurice Collis, Marco Polo, Collier's Encyclopedia, vol.15, p.383)

After Marco Polo's era, it seemed there was no direct contact between China and Western countries until the end of the Ming Dynasty, when missionaries traveled east one after another. Exchanges between China and the West then reached an unprecedented level.

Francis Xavier, a Spanish Jesuit, was the first to come to China, but failed to enter inland China. Matteo Ricci was the first Jesuit who successfully came into inland China and spread gospel. Ricci was born in Italy in 1552. He joined the Society of Jesus, an organization within the Roman Catholic Church, at the age of 19, and in 1577, he was allowed to preach in the Far East. The following March, together with 14 other Jesuits, he started from Lisbon and in September reached Goa, a Portuguese colony in India. He did missionary work in India and Jiao Zhi (present-day Vietnam) for four years.

In August 1582 (the tenth year of Emperor Wanli, the Ming Dynasty), Matteo Ricci was sent to China as a missionary. He first arrived in Macao, where he learnt Chinese. In 1584, he came to

Zhaoqing, Guangdong Province, with another priest, Michele de Ruggieri. They did not preach on a large scale in the beginning, but invested much of their time and energy in studying the Chinese language as well as local etiquette and conventions. In this way they sought to gain the trust of the Chinese, especially that of the officials. Dressed in Buddhist robes, they claimed to be from India, and called the church they'd established "Xianhua Temple" to make people think they were Buddhists. They also used atlases, star-disks, and prisms and other novel Western things to attract people, taking this opportunity to promote Catholic doctrines.

In the summer of 1589, Matteo Ricci arrived in Shaozhou, where he made friends with a scholar named Qu Taisu, from whom he learned the Four Books (the *Great Learning*, the *Doctrine of the Mean*, the *Analects of Confucius* and *Mencius*) and the *Five Classics* (the *Book of Songs*, the *Book of History,* the *Book of Changes,* the *Book of Rites* and the *Spring and Autumn Annals).* Qu Taisu enthusiastically publicized Ricci and his work, and the latter consciously mingled with local officials, presenting them with such Western items as astronomical instruments, globes, and sundials. Thus, his reputation spread gradually in the locality. After a long period of observation, he found that the social status of Buddhist monks was far lower than that of scholars. So from 1594, he changed to wear Confucian-style clothing.

In 1595, Matteo Ricci got to Nanchang, and on September 22 the next year, he successfully forecasted a solar eclipse, a feat that won him considerable fame. Here, he associated with many bureaucratic literati and became a popular figure. Consequently, he was appointed as person-in-charge of the Jesuit parish for China, solely responsible for missionary activities in the country. His church also instructed him to think of ways to go to Beijing to present himself before the Emperor of China, so that the word of Jesus might be

Matteo Ricci

spread, and missionary work in China protected in the future. The church also sent, via Macao, many gifts prepared for the emperor. Soon afterwards, Matteo Ricci had the opportunity of following Wang Zhongming—Minister of the Board of Rites of Nanjing— to Beijing. Ricci returned to Nanjing soon after, and here he made friends with many celebrated people, including Xu Guangqi, who was to offer him the biggest help later. With their support, Matteo Ricci established a church in Nanjing, and the place where he lived became a church as well. Thereafter, Nanjing became one of the most important Catholic missionary centers in China.

On January 24, 1601, Matteo Ricci came to Beijing again with Diego de Pantoja, and presented Emperor Shenzong of the Ming Dynasty with gifts such as an automatic clock, copies of the *Bible*, a world atlas, dulcimers and so on. Shenzong was very pleased, and allowed Matteo Ricci and others to live in Beijing permanently by an imperial edict. Taking advantage of his rich knowledge of the East and West, Matteo Ricci associated extensively with the Chinese bureaucratic literati, and attracted some of them to the Catholic Church. By 1605, he had developed 200 followers, including several dukes and ministers.

Matteo Ricci's success was based on two factors: first, thanks to his knowledge of the natural sciences and items of novelty, he won the goodwill of the Chinese people. Second, he did not stick to Catholic rules in the course of his missionary work; dressed in Confucian clothes, he took on a tolerant and understanding attitude toward traditional Chinese customs. He allowed China's Catholics to continue their traditional worship of heaven, ancestors and Confucius, and used the Confucian classics to explain Catholic doctrines. Later missionaries followed his strategies, known as the Matteo Ricci Rules.

Matteo Ricci wrote more than 20 kinds of books, and made

many contributions to the spread of subjects such as astronomy, mathematics, geography, architecture, painting, music and so on. It can be said that he was a pioneer of East-West knowledge transmission. His *A Panoramic Map of Countries in the World* was the first world map in China's history, and was block-printed 12 successive times in China. On May 11, 1610, Matteo Ricci died of illness in Beijing, and the emperor granted him a burial in the western suburb of the city (a place in what is now the School of the Beijing Municipal Committee).

Matteo Ricci paved the way to China for other missionaries. Following in his footsteps, they came in an endless stream and scattered in all directions. The Catholic Church expanded its influence all over China with unprecedented momentum. Other influential missionaries included Johann Adam Schall von Bell (German, 1591-1666), Ferdinandus Verbiest (Belgian, 1623-1688), Giuseppe Castiglione (Italian, 1688-1766) and so on.

Schall arrived in China in 1622 during the late Ming Dynasty.

Ferdinandus Verbiest

Xu Guangqi, a minister of the Catholic faith, appointed him to an important position: his work would be to help Xu Guangqi revise calendars. Together they finished compiling the *Chongzhen Calendar*. After the fall of the Ming Dynasty, the newly established Qing Dynasty continued to give him prominence by conferring upon him official positions in court. However, the mushrooming of missionary forces caused some discontent among some Chinese officials. Led by minister Yang Guangxian, they carried out attacks against Schall and other missionaries; he was once even arrested and jailed.

After Emperor Kangxi (who reigned from

1662 to 1722) came into power, he decided to use the experimental method to distinguish the pros and cons of Chinese and Western calendars. By now Schall had succumbed to an illness, and so Emperor Kangxi ordered his aide, Ferdinandus' Verbiest—who had arrived in China, in 1659, at the beginning of the Qing Dynasty— and Yang Guangxian to test the calendars in public. Ferdinandus' was the accurate one, whereas Yang Guangxian was off the mark every time. Emperor Kangxi recalled Yang from his post and asked Ferdinandus to be in charge of the Board of Astronomy. Henceforth, Western missionaries would go on to control the Board of Astronomy for a long time. Giuseppe Castiglione (who arrived in China in 1715, the 54th year of Emperor Qianlong) served as a court painter for a long period, and participated in the construction of the famous Yuanmingyuan (the Old Summer Palace), having also designed the Western Storied Buildings. He was then promoted to a 3rd grade court official.

The missionaries also taught Western sciences, including astronomy, mathematics, geography, physics, firearm manufacturing and so on. They also served the Chinese government by translating books, revising calendars, manufacturing artillery, mapping and so on. Scores of Chinese learnt from the missionaries, their interest in Western knowledge much greater than religious enthusiasm. Xu Guangqi (1562-1633), a minister during the Ming Dynasty, was a scientist himself. He imbibed Western ideas in Europe, and together with Matteo Ricci, co-translated Euclid's *The Elements*. Emperor Kangxi of the Qing Dynasty often consulted missionaries around him. Not only did he study astronomy and geography, but also had a profound knowledge of physics, chemistry and advanced mathematics.

French missionary Jean de Fontaney wrote in a domestic letter, "When the priests explained something to the emperor, he understood easily. He studied enthusiastically and would not suspend his lessons even when he went to Changchun Park, which was two French miles away from Beijing. So the priests had to go there every day, no matter what the weather was like."

With the road paved by Matteo Ricci, the spread of Catholicism went on very smoothly. Some of the people in the Society of Jesus, as well as Franciscan and Dominican missionaries who came to China later, did not agree with Matteo Ricci's methods. They were opposed to the Chinese people's Confucian and ancestor worship, and this controversy in China later extended to the Holy See in Rome. In 1705 and 1720, the pope Klein Mans 11 sent special envoys to China, prohibiting the Chinese from worshiping Heaven, Confucius or their ancestors, and requesting Emperor Kangxi to order them to obey the Holy See. Kangxi did not take lightly to the Holy See's interference in China's internal affairs, and prohibited any further spread of Catholicism in the country. Later emperors such as Yongzheng and Qianlong continued to implement this policy of banning religions, and the Society of Jesus soon disappeared from the scene, after having taken root in China for almost 200 years.

Today the graves of Matteo Ricci, Johann Adam Schall von Bell, Ferdinandus Verbiest, Guiseppe Castiglione, etc., are considered Beijing heritage sites, and are fully protected.

Ancient China was not self-enclosed. It opened its arms to the outside world and assimilated the best things from other civilizations. In the process, it strengthened ties with other peoples and enriched its own culture. China became conservative only during the middle of the Qing Dynasty, when the rulers were ignorant of the world situation. Running on both blind arrogance and fear of foreign invasion, they implemented a closed-door policy, which led to modern China's lag behind western countries.

Chapter 9

Door Opened by Cannons

Human society saw unprecedented changes in the middle of the 19th century. The modernization drive in Europe and North America had just begun and was gaining momentum, leading to an unforeseen historic trend. Due to its extended isolation, China was weak and poor at the time. However, its large market potential and rich resources were attractive to and were coveted by the European and American powers, namely, Britain, America, France, Germany, Russia, and Italy, as well as its close neighbor to the east, Japan. Powers entered China one after another, staking out their "sphere of influence" for their own interest. What could China do in response to these major upheavals, unprecedented for the past three thousand years?

1. McCartney Hits a Wall in China

During the Ming Dynasty, feudal rulers adopted strict policies prohibiting maritime trade or contact with foreign countries. The rulers in the early period of Qing Dynasty (1644-1911) also continued such policies until the late 17th century, when Emperor Kangxi, who was quite a visionary, temporarily relaxed the ban. Customs offices were established in the provinces of Guangdong, Fujian, Zhejiang and Jiangsu for trading with foreign merchants. In 1686, the Guangdong authorities enlisted 13 relatively powerful businessmen and appointed them to conduct trade with foreign merchants on foreign ships, as well as levy tariffs for the customs office.

Thanks to the reigns of Emperor Kangxi and Emperor Yongzheng, Emperor Qianlong took over a China which had entered a prosperous age.

However, despite the glory on the surface, the massive state machinery was showing more and more cracks with increasingly evident symptoms of decline. Emperor Qianlong was himself a

Huangpu Port, Guangzhou, early location of foreign business houses

show-off and liked seeking empty glory. To equal his grandfather Emperor Kangxi's historical accomplishment, and stamp his name on the pages of history, Emperor Qianlong followed his grandfather's footsteps by conducting as many as six inspection tours to southern China.

Even today, a number of legends circulate about these tours. One legend has it that Emperor Qianlong saw some village girls picking tea leaves at the foot of Shifeng Hill in Longjing (dragon well) area of Hangzhou. To display his concern for people's living conditions, he also joined the chore. However, just as he started picking, a eunuch reported, "The empress dowager is ill, please return to Beijing immediately." Not daring to delay a moment, he unconsciously put a handful of tea leaves he had picked into his own pocket and rushed back to Beijing without rest on the way. Actually his mother was simply troubled by a minor discomfort caused by excessive heat in the liver, which had led to swollen eyes accompanied by a stomach ache. When Emperor Qianlong met her, she smelt an invigorating aroma, and thinking it might be a gift her son had brought for her from the south, she inquired about it. Emperor Qianlong felt quite embarrassed as he had forgotten about the gift in the rush. Then where did the fragrance come from? He searched his own clothes and found in his pocket the handful of tea leaves he had picked at Shifeng Hill of Hangzhou. The refreshing smell was from the leaves that had dried after several days. The empress expressed a desire to taste them, and Emperor Qianlong ordered his maids to prepare a pot of tea with these leaves. The tea served to the empress dowager had a sweet and pleasant scent, and serenaded her nostrils. After drinking it she felt much better and said, "Hangzhou's dragon well tea is really wonderful and a miraculous medicine."

Seeing her exult about it, Emperor Qianlong handed down

an imperial edict right away, conferring upon the 18 tea trees at the foot of Shifeng Hill the title of imperial tea. Since then, every harvest of the trees was taken to the empress dowager as a tribute. Today, the 18 tea trees still grow in front of Hugong Temple at Longjing (dragon well) Village, Hangzhou. The stories about Emperor Qianlong's incognito trips to south of the Yangtze River have been adapted and made into a very popular prime-time program on TV, which is broadcast across the country. This reflects the desire of the Chinese people to learn more about their leadership.

However, Qianlong's travels to the south were extremely expensive. A number of temporary imperial palaces were constructed along his travel routes from Beijing to Hangzhou. The southern inspection fleet consisted of more than one thousand ships at a time. All localities along the way had to prepare food, stock water and anything else they needed. Despite Emperor Qianlong's orders to prevent wastage of money, local officials still tried every means possible to please him. He conducted six southern inspection tours in his lifetime, with each costlier than the previous ones. It mounted a heavy burden on the people, and in the end, ate up the treasury of the dynasty. There were indeed some clear-headed officials in Qing courts, who tried to dissuade him from these tours. However, Emperor Qianlong reprimanded them severely, not realizing the mistake until the last few years of his life.

He said, "I believe I did not commit major wrong doings during my 60 years as the emperor, except for the six southern inspection tours that wasted much money and resources and burdened the people. The goodwill did not translate into good outcomes."

After that no emperor in Qing Dynasty embarked on southern inspection tours modeled on the Qianlong ones. It was also because

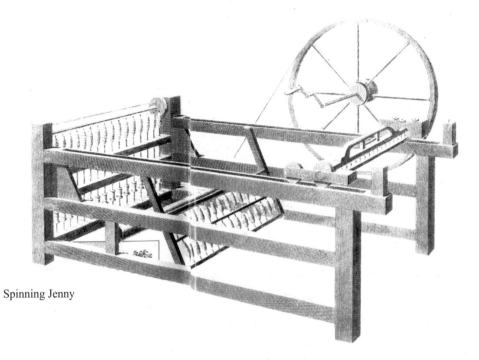

Spinning Jenny

the treasury of the Qing court could no longer afford it.

Emperor Qianlong had always felt like the center of the universe, feeling no necessity to have contact with the outside world. In the later stages of his reign, he resumed the prohibition of maritime trade, pushing China back to isolation.

At the same time, the Western world was experiencing epoch-making changes. In the 30th year of Emperor Qianlong's reign (1765), a British textile worker Hargreaves invented a new type of weaving machine, the Spinning Jenny, which greatly improved the efficiency of weaving machines, leading to Britain kicking off its industrial revolution. In the 50th year of Emperor Qianlong's reign (1785), Watt improved the steam engine. Bolton invented the steamship soon after; an Englishman named Stephenson invented steam locomotives. These new revolutionary improvements in productivity pushed western society to develop at a very rapid

pace, leading it to enter a time of colonial expansion and depreda-
tion in search of resources worldwide.

In the 40th year of Emperor Qianlong's reign (1775), the
American Civil War broke out. The United States became independent and the *Human Rights Act* was ratified eight years later.
In the 54th year of Emperor Qianlong's reign (1789), the French
revolution took place, which led to the issuance of the *Declara-
tion of Human Rights* and the capital punishment for Louis XVI.
All these major events gave birth to the creation of a new level of
productivity and a new political system. The geopolitical structure
of the world had profoundly changed, generating a huge impact on
the world's history.

In desperate search for markets, the emerging capitalist
western countries were eager to trade with China, which had a
large territory and a big population. However, the Qing Dynasty
declined foreign trade and had its doors tightly closed, due to its
dislike of Western cultures.

First steam locomotive

Despite the fact that by the mid 18th century Britain was the largest Western trader with China, its industrial products saw a cold shoulder in China's self-sufficient economy, and bilateral trade was limited to Britain's purchase of Chinese teas with silver. The British were deeply troubled by the increasingly large trade deficit and urgently needed to open the closed door of the Qing Empire.

The British king George III made a major decision in September 1792. He dispatched an embassy to the remote and ancient country of China, headed by Lord George McCartney, with a large fleet composed of Royal British warships, including *The Lion, The Hindoostan,* and *The Jackal*. The delegation was sent on the pretext of commemorating the Emperor's 83rd birthday, with which they wanted to open the Chinese market.

The British diplomatic mission arrived in China in May 1793 (the 5th year of Emperor Qianlong's reign). While waiting for the

Emperor Qianlong Meeting British Ambassador Mc-Cartney and His Party, by British painter William Alexander

provincial governor of Liangguang (Guangdong and Guangxi) to report their visit to the throne, they anchored their ships off the shore of Macao. Emperor Qianlong was extremely pleased to learn of the visit of the British diplomatic mission, and appointed senior officials specially for receiving the diplomatic mission.

When the British diplomatic mission heard of the imperial edict, they left Macao for the northern port of Tianjin. From there they reached Beijing through the Great Canal. After brief refreshments, McCartney led his people to travel another 200 kilometers beyond the Great Wall for the Chengde Summer Palace, where the 83-year-old Emperor's birthday party was to be held.

The Qing government attached extraordinary importance to this visit. Emperor Qianlong had directed the Privy Council (equivalent of a cabinet) to draft a reception proposal, including official court audience with the Emperor, granting of presents, a banquet, theatre and sightseeing etc. When McCartney and his mission arrived at Chengde in September 1793, Emperor Qianlong had been waiting for long, perched on his throne, courting a gesture which suggested he was the mandate of the heaven, the center of the world, and the inferior tributary states had all come to pay respect to him.

As both sides prepared for the meeting with great interest and enthusiasm, an unpleasant thing occurred—the two sides got into a serious disagreement over the formality of the court audience with the emperor. The Qing tradition provided that foreign envoys must kowtow before the Qing Emperor with the full formality including "three kneel-downs on both knees and nine kowtows each time". But McCartney believed that the full formality would harm the dignity of the British Empire and suggested bending down with one knee would be more appropriate.

Emperor Qianlong was furious at the suggestion. He deemed

McCartney and his mission as envoys who could not have come to pay tributes, as his agreeing to entertain them itself was a huge honor to them. He could not imagine the British mission could be so insensitive to this. Emperor Qianlong told his official, "I am not happy with the arrogance of the British. Such uncultivated people from remote regions do not deserve preferential treatment."

The British mission could now possibly be expelled, and McCartney would have to return without accomplishing the assignment he had been sent for. After careful deliberations, he offered his counter conditions for accepting the kowtow formality, which included a reciprocal formality when a Chinese envoy visited Britain, and a Chinese official kneeling down to the portrait of the British king. The two sides finally reached an agreement with concessions. The British envoy would perform the British-style formality in the banquet and the complete kowtow formality for the Emperor's birthday gala.

Emperor Qianlong also softened his attitude. He thought these people were from a remote maritime state and might not be familiar with the regulations of his celestial dynasty. Since they were now submissive, he thought he could still bestow upon them his imperial kindness and benefactions.

Emperor Qianlong also let a key senior member of his Privy Council, He Shen, accompany the mission for sightseeing, including a tour around the imperial garden.

During the official celebration of the emperor's "ten thousand years of longevity", McCartney presented gifts to the emperor, including telescopes, clocks, warship models and modern firearms. The obsession and pride of being the "celestial dynasty" made the emperor and his officials disregard these highly technical devices as worthless, and the gifts were made display items in the Forbidden City, Garden of Perfection and Brightness, and other imperial gardens. When the British offered to show how the firearms worked, the officials declined, saying there was nothing new and it did not matter whether they worked or not. Ironically, the Qing officials finally tasted the power of the British firearms 48 years later in 1848.

According to the principle of largesse and past practices, Emperor Qianlong in his turn gifted thousands of pieces of silk, porcelains, jades and handicrafts to McCartney and his mission.

According to the Qing provision, foreign envoys were not allowed to stay in Beijing for more than 40 days. Hence, McCartney's request to remain until after the Spring Festival was turned down. By then the British king's letter to Qianlong had been translated and submitted to the throne. The letter was titled "The King of Great Britain Asks the Chinese Emperor to Give Positive Considerations to the Requests Raised by His Special Envoy." McCartney had raised the following requests: relaxation of restrictions on trade between Britain and China; the acquisition by Britain of "a small unfortified island near Guangzhou for the residence of British traders, storage of goods, and outfitting of ships"; establishment of a permanent British embassy in Beijing; reduction or elimination of tariffs for imports from Britain; permission for British missionaries to preach freely in China.

Emperor Qianlong was extremely angry after reading the letter, particularly that the British envoy turned out to have other intentions besides paying tribute. He rejected the British request of acquiring a small island for British traders. He said that the entire Chinese territory was within clearly defined Chinese borders, including islands and sandbanks. How could they be allowed to be lined out at will? He also criticized the other contents of the letter in a reply letter given to McCartney before his embassy was rushed to depart.

Qianlong's rejection of the British request marked the failure of the mission and their last hopes were dashed to the ground. Emperor Qianlong appointed special officials to convey the British mission to leave Beijing, and also ordered local officials along the route to prevent the British from making trouble.

The McCartney mission had failed. But this contact helped the two large countries to gain some basic understanding about each other. In particular, Britain learnt more about the crisis lurking over the Qing Empire under the cover of a so-called prosperous age. McCartney said, "The Qing Empire is like a decaying first class warship. The hard work of a group of vigilant and diligent captains has kept it afloat for the past 150 years. The size and exterior of the ship is the only place where it outdoes neighboring ships. There will be no discipline or safety once there is no capable director on the deck." In the same period, J.G. Herder (1744-1803), a German philosopher and historian wrote, "This empire is a mummy smeared with antiseptics, painted with ideographs and then wrapped in a piece of silk. However, the blood circulation in its body has already stopped, just like a hibernating animal. This is why it peeks, blocks and isolates itself from everything of the outside world. Without any understanding or passion of the outside world, it is enmeshed all the time in a priggishness of itself."

After Qianlong's death, the British king again sent McCartney on a mission to China. However, Emperor Jiaqing, the son of Emperor Qianlong, gave a far more subdued reception to the British mission, resulting in relations going cold between the two countries. The British understood that normal trade between the two countries could not be realized, and took to opium smuggling on a large scale.

The Opium War broke out in 1840, during which the British imperialists opened China's door with cannons and gunneries. The

Qing government was forced to sign the humiliating Sino-British Nanjing Treaty in July 1842, exactly half a century after the first visit by a British mission to China. The British army eventually obtained with cast-iron ships and big guns what the British mission wished to gain through pleasantries during the time of Emperor Qianlong.

2. Opium Trade Led to War

Since foreign trade in the Qing Dynasty was only allowed in Guangzhou, Britain and other western capitalist countries found it difficult to sell their products and make exorbitant profits within that one area. Therefore, opium became the first "product" they sold to China.

Opium is a narcotic made from the latex released by lacerating the immature seed pods of opium poppies. Taking a little of it

Opium smokers

can ease pain, and relieve diarrhea and cough. However, it is also highly addictive, leading to emaciation and eventual death.

After the British troops' occupation of India, they forced the local people to plant opium poppy on a large scale. Then the East India Company, the British colonial organization, collected the opium and transported it to China. The Qing government issued the decree of banning the transportation and consumption of opium many times, but the smuggling of opium kept increasing since many officials themselves were addicted to opium.

In 1800, 4,500 cases of opium were shipped into China, and the quantity increased year by year. By 1838, it had increased to over 40,000 cases. Meanwhile, the number of Chinese who consumed opium also increased tremendously. In 1835, there were 2 million people consuming the drug, with 4.2 million *liang* (15.96 million grams) silver flowing out. The opium not only did great harm to the Chinese people, but also brought huge losses to the finances of the Qing Dynasty. However, the British businessmen were not satisfied with this trade volume. In order to earn more profits and increase their financial income, they began to stir up wars. In 1832, British Foreign Secretary Palmerton advocated that the British government launch a war on China in order to improve the "opium trade".

The Qing government had three different attitudes towards the opium trade—prohibition of opium, relaxed prohibition, and anti-prohibition. Some righteous officials advocated banning the drug, and Lin Zexu was one of the most determined of these officials.

Lin Zexu was incorruptible and had

Lin Zexu

a better understanding of the western world. He submitted a letter to Emperor Daoguang, warning that if opium consumption was not banned, China would have no soldiers left to resist foreign occupation nor the money to support the army. Emperor Daoguang was touched by Lin Zexu's declamation and decided to ban the consumption of opium. In December 1838, Lin Zexu was appointed the Imperial Commissioner to Guangzhou by Emperor Daoguang, mainly in charge of the ban.

In January, 1839, Lin Zexu arrived in Guangzhou, brimming with confidence. Upon arrival, he changed into a civilian dress and immediately stepped out to make investigations. He found that the health of many people had been seriously damaged by opium intake and they were too weak to even stand a gust of wind, leave alone being capable of work. Thus, towns and villages had dilapidated with people living in destitution. Lin Zexu believed that in order to ban opium thoroughly, they must make adjustments from the inside. They must seriously punish those merchants and corrupt officials who smuggled opium and lured the civilians.

A few days later, Lin Zexu went to investigate the Academy House as the Imperial Commissioner and held an examination. In the question paper given out, students found a slip of paper, saying: "In this exam, you may not answer the questions on the paper, but you must write down the names and addresses of the opium smugglers you know and their activities. You need to specify the inside story of the bribery and the smuggling of the opium, and are not allowed to conceal anything." Students in this Academy House came from various places and knew a lot about the trade. In addition, most of them, young and enthusiastic, had a deep-seated hatred of opium smuggling and therefore wrote down all they knew on the paper.

Lin Zexu finally learnt all about opium smuggling and strictly punished some soldiers and opium smugglers who had violated the laws. After that, he issued a proclamation demanding that the foreign businessmen surrender all the opium within three days and write a guarantee that they would never smuggle opium from then on. If any opium was found in the future, the opium would be confiscated and the person possessing it would be sentenced to death according to the laws.

After the news spread, opium smugglers were flustered, with some of them surrendering the opium. The British superintendent Charles Elliot, who lived in Macao, rushed to Guangzhou to tell the opium smugglers not to be afraid and that the British naval vessels were near the shores, which would help them escape at any time. Chinese employees of the foreign companies learnt of this plot and when Elliot was planning to help several big opium smugglers escape, hundreds of Chinese workers encircled them. The news soon reached Lin Zexu, who was excited to hear that Chinese workers were voluntarily fighting against opium smugglers. He made an announcement that he would not leave Guangzhou unless opium smuggling was terminated. He would not give up halfway.

Lin Zexu then issued an order that the opium trade between China and Britain had to stop. He threatened to send troops to seal off the foreign companies, withdraw the Chinese workers working in them and cut off transportation from their offices to the sea, and if they resisted, food supply would be cut off immediately. When Elliot learnt about the order, he was already at his wits' end. British merchants then surrendered the opium, over 20,000 cases in total (including over 1,500 cases belonging to American merchants), weighing about 1.185 million kilograms.

To demonstrate his resolve to prohibit opium trade, Lin Zexu decided to destroy the confiscated opium. On June 3, 1839, Lin Zexu led officials from all across Guangdong Province to a plateau near Humen beach and supervised the destruction of the opium in person.

As the destruction of the opium began, large groups of bare-chested workers and soldiers carried the opium cases on their shoulders to the plateau. After laying down the cases, they hacked them open, chopped the opium into pieces and threw them into a large brine pond. Wooden planks were then set afloat over the pond, and workers standing on them scattered lime into the mix, and with spades began churning it. Soon, the mix began emitting smoke as the opium oil started decomposing and the opium slag sank. The air was filled with a putrid smell, as the slag was then dumped into the sea. It took more than 20 days to destroy the entire lot.

The foreign merchants, invited by Lin Zexu to witness the opium turn into slag and flow into the sea, lowered their heads. Lin Zexu said to them: The prohibition is to ban the poisonous opium, which is not a legal trade. We would welcome it if you carry out trade with due respect for the law of our country.

When the news spread to Britain, British authorities were livid. China's opium prohibition "provides us an opportunity to declare war", they thought, and claimed that China's prohibition was "aggressive behavior" towards Britain. In October 1839, the British government decided to send troops to China. In February, 1840, the British government formed an "East Expedition Army" comprising military vessels, transport ships and armed steam-boats with 540 cannons and 4,000 soldiers. The Army set off in June 1840 to Guangdong and Macao. On June 28, British vessels encircled the seaport of the Pearl River and the Opium War broke out.

As the British army was not familiar with China's sea route, it was necessary for them to hire Chinese to lead them. Lin Zexu, therefore, requested the local fishermen to cooperate with China's naval forces, so that they could sneak in on the British vessels and set them ablaze. As a result, many British soldiers were burnt to death and drowned. The British troops found Guangdong heavily guarded and could take little advantage of it. Hence, they sailed north. On July 5, 1840, they seized Dinghai district of Zhejiang Province and ransacked the city. Since most of the northern naval defenses were out of use, the British troops quickly seized Dagukou in Tianjin, thereby threatening to overrun Jingshi (the present capital, Beijing).

British invaders then sent a memorandum to the Qing government in accordance with a pre-fixed schedule, making a series of unreasonable requests such as legalization of opium trade, and payment of indemnities and cession of territories. Emperor Daoguang, who himself was not keen on opium prohibition, panicked and hurriedly sent Qishan to Tianjin port to negotiate with the British. During the negotiations, Qishan attributed all the "faults" to Lin Zexu and guaranteed to condemn him. Qishan also assured the British in private that as long as they withdrew to Guangzhou, all their demands would be accepted in the negotiations there. The British troops therefore began to pull back to the south from Tianjin in September. The fatuous Emperor Daoguang thought Qishan had rendered meritorious service to the country, appointed him the Imperial Commissioner to Guangzhou and continued to negotiate with the British troops. He also dismissed Lin Zexu.

Prior to Qishan's arrival at Guangzhou, British invaders had already prepared for a war in order to raise their bargaining chips. In December, the negotiations began. Elliot demanded a cash indemnity of 20 million taels of silver for the confiscated opium, cession of an island to Britain, opening of more ports to the

Western world, allowing foreigners to open trading companies, and payment of indemnities to Britain for the military spending on the war. Qishan tried to bargain with him, and for the cession said he did not have the right to decide, but promised to make a request to Emperor Daoguang. When the British realized they could not get what they wanted, they turned to military measures to force China.

In January 1841, the British troops seized two fortresses guarding Humen. Humen was in imminent danger. General Guan Tianpei and the defender of Humen Fort had no alternative but to ask for relief. However, Qishan refused to help him. When Guan Tianpei's messenger repeated the request, Qishan replied perfunctorily: "I will send 200 soldiers secretly." However, when the messenger insisted he would not leave without substantial relief, Qishan shouted at him ruthlessly and angrily: "Going to Humen means death. I will not send even one more soldier." Guan Tianpei, upon learning this, had no choice but to fight the powerful British troops alone and make a last-ditch defense.

Qishan then sent messengers to Elliot requesting him to resume negotiations secretly. This made Elliot behave aggressively and he asked Qishan to accept all his demands. Left with little choice, Qishan agreed verbally to draft the Convention of Chuanbi, which stipulated China's cession of Hong Kong and its ports to Britain, payment of six million yuan for the opium, opening of Guangzhou port for trade, etc. Eventually, the British troops did seize Hong Kong.

When Emperor Daoguang learnt of the proposal, he felt that to cede territory and pay indemnities seriously damaged "the dignity of the Qing Dynasty" and instead decided to declare war on Britain. He appointed his nephew Yishan the "General to put down usurpers" (General Jingni) and assembled 17,000 soldiers from all the provinces to send them to Guangzhou to fight the British troops. However, earlier in the latter half of February, Elliot had led 18 British naval vessels to seize Humen Fort. Naval commander Guan Tianpei tried to defend the fort, but due to disparity in the number of vessels and soldiers, Guan Tianpei and over 400 soldiers sacrificed their lives. After Humen was occupied, British troops seized the advantage, intruded into inland waters and Guangdong was finally completely opened to the Western world.

Two months after Humen was occupied, Yishan led his troops to Guangzhou. After arriving there, he naively decided to divide his men into three groups and ordered them to attack the British army at night in an attempt to triumph over it by good accident. As a result, Yishan's troops were dispersed, and easily routed by British troops. Yishan fled back into the city in panic and the four forts in the four important strongholds were lost without even a fight. They stood high and the British bombarded Guangzhou from them day and night. Yishan and his fellowmen were frightened and hoisted a white flag in front of the city wall to appease the British, even sending messengers to beg Elliot to stop the assault. On May 27, 1841, Yishan accepted the five terms posed by Elliot and signed

The Treaty of Nanjing was signed by China and Britain aboard the British warship *Cornwallis*.

the Guangzhou Treaty. The treaty stipulated that six million yuan should be paid within one week in order to redeem the city from the British troops, and another 300,000 yuan ($42,900) to compensate the losses of the Western merchants. Also, Yishan should lead his troop 60 *li* (30 kilometers) out of Guangzhou.

The British troops took advantage of this miscalculation, and extended the war, expecting to take more advantage. By August 26 that year, the British troops had seized Xiamen, Dinghai, Wusongkou of Shanghai and Zhenjiang, and arrived at the Yangtze River near Nanjing. On August 29, threatened by the British troops, the Qing government signed the first unequal treaty in Chinese history—the Treaty of Nanjing. The main content of the treaty was: the island of Hong Kong was ceded to Britain; five ports were opened for trade—Guangzhou, Xiamen, Fuzhou, Ningbo and Shanghai; the British government was paid 21 million yuan in total; Taxation on import and export good of Britain in China be discussed by both countries. British merchants could trade freely with Chinese merchants without limitation of the Cohong (an organization established in Guangzhou in 1760 to monopolize trade,

Hong Kong in 1860

squash competition and disadvantage foreign trade).

Eventually, the war caused by opium trade ended with the defeat of the Qing government. China was forced by Western gunboats to open to the outside world. The Qing government had gradually lost its political and economical independence, and had become dependent on the Western powers. To cede territory and pay indemnities thereafter became the most common diplomatic behavior of the Qing government.

Chapter 10

Awakening, Reform and Revolution

The defeat in the Opium War (1840-1842) gradually led Chinese society into a semi-colonial and semi-feudal state. The Chinese people, hoodwinked by extended seclusion and isolation, were forced to experience the outside world on their own. The fire at Yuanmingyuan (the Garden of Perfection and Brightness, or the old Summer Palace) burnt down the Qing Dynasty rulers' illusory sense of superiority. Development and reform had become the only options for self-emancipation. However, the fatuous Empress Dowager Cixi (1835-1908) refused to embrace change and personally snuffed off the reforms. The opportunities for the Qing Dynasty (1644-1911) to defend itself was squandered by its rulers, and the future belonged to the Chinese who had been awakened and were carrying out revolutions. Sun Yat-sen was one such forerunner.

1. Opening One's Eyes to the World

In the Opium War, the Qing Dynasty, claiming to be the "Celestial Dynasty and the Superior Nation", was beaten hollow and was forced to sign humiliating agreements that required territorial cession and reparation. The time of peace had come to an end and some intellectuals started having a sense of crisis regarding the nation. They took the lead in breaking the narrow mentality of isolation, and began casting their eyes on the rest of the world.

Lin Zexu was the first in early modern Chinese history to have a sense of the outside world. Lin Zexu's idea of the world was not an inherent quality but a sensibility formed through dealing with foreigners, particularly the British colonialists. In the beginning, Lin too had a lot of misunderstandings. For instance, in a memorial he submitted to the throne in September 1839, he said, "The barbarian soldiers, except for advantages with gunnery and firearms, are not skillful in close combat or in their foot movements. With leg gaiters tightly wrapped, their legs have difficulty in flexion and curl. Once on shore, their movement would be stunted and hence their strength is not beyond control." This was at the time a popular misunderstanding that the gaiters wrapped around the foreigners' legs prevented them from bending, and so the foreigners were only good at sea warfare and could not accomplish anything once they come onto shore. As for the foreigners' cast-iron ships and big guns, Lin Zexu once held opinions like these, "The British will have to come in boats to attack China. If they dare to sail into our inland rivers, their ships will be left stranded and keeled as the tides ebb. Secondly, they won't have enough food storage. Thirdly, they lack sufficient munitions. Hence, they will be like fish lying on a dry river, awaiting their doom." He also believed the foreigners were addicted to eating lamb and beef. Therefore, he thought they would die of indigestion in the absence of tea or rhubarb imported from China. These are obviously misunderstandings about "barbarian outsiders".

However, Lin Zexu improved his perceptions and became more practical and realistic about the "barbarians" after further personal experiences. It is said that some foreign merchants in Guangzhou wanted to become acquainted and establish underhand connections with Lin, just a few days after his arrival to the city as Imperial Commissioner. However, contrary to their expectations, they found Lin's attitude to be quite firm. These foreign businessmen then planted a trick on Lin. One day, they invited Lin to a banquet in which a "foreign dish" was served towards the end. Lin and the other invited Chinese officials saw a light mist hovering over the dish, and thinking it must be hot, blew on it before drawing a spoonful into their mouths. But they were surprised to find it freezing cold, and could not help the shiver that went down their spines. The foreigners burst out laughing. The dish was what we know so well today as "ice-cream". The Chinese people are always concerned about face saving. As a court official, Lin certainly thought it to be a disgrace. He then planned a counter trick when he returned the hospitality. He ordered a famous dish from the Fujian and Taiwan areas—*Taiji Yuni* (The Ultimate Mashed Taro). It was not served until the foreign merchants became quite hungry. When it was presented, they saw a colorful decoration with the nice *Taiji* pattern on top. It smelt great and did not give out steam. So they thought it was a cold dessert. Being hungry, the foreigners put a spoonful of taro into their mouths. What they did not know is that sugar and pork fat had been added to the taro, hence it was not giving out steam even while being very hot. Their mouths and lips hurt, the foreign merchants yelled out in pain. Though this helped to even matters, it also broadened Lin's vision. Traditional Chinese experience said that stuff that gives off "mist" must be hot. Lin hadn't thought these foreigners could make such "cold" food. He gradually began to realize that the foreigners' knowledge and insight was different from that of the Chinese.

Lin Zexu had hernia. He fell ill with it again during his time in Guangdong where he had come for opium ban. His subordinates in Guangdong were very concerned. They suggested Western medication and recommended the American doctor Peter Parker. Dr. Parker had graduated from the University of Yale and had arrived in Guangzhou on the commercial boat *Morrison* in 1835. Thereafter he opened a clinic named Xing Dou Lan. Even though the people in Guangzhou were used to Chinese medication, out of curiosity they tried some of the little pills prescribed by Dr. Parker. To their surprise, their illness was quickly treated and they began to feel the benefits of Western medicine. After this, Dr. Parker's fame spread wide, and many in Guangzhou came to consult him about their diseases.

Lin Zexu was focused on war-and-peace diplomacy, and frequently dealt with the British for it. At that critical moment, he did not think it appropriate to see a foreign doctor. But his condition deteriorated critically. After careful consideration, Lin wrote a letter to Dr. Parker asking for a "prescription for hernia", thinking that Western medical methods were similar to those of the Chinese. Dr. Parker wrote back politely, attaching an anthroponomical drawing. He advised that the patient come for the hernia band personally. However, Lin Zexu was not willing to go to a Western clinic as he was an Imperial Commissioner. Later, he learned about a person with the same illness who had been bounded with the hernia band. Lin then sent this person to the clinic for the same band. He was turned down. Dr. Parker told him the hernia band could only be used by the doctor. Having thought further, Lin sent another hernia patient to the clinic where Dr. Parker bound him with the hernia band. The patient felt much better. Lin was hence convinced that the Western medical methods had genuine efficacy and was more eager to relieve himself from the pain with the help of a hernia band.

One day a patient came to Dr. Parker and identified himself as the brother of the commissioner Lin Zexu, who had exactly the same figure and measurements as him. "The band that fits me will definitely fit my brother," the person said. Faced with the traditional ways of medical consultation with the Chinese, Dr. Parker had to make an exception. He wrote on the patient card, "Patient number: 6565; Illness: hernia; Name: Lin Zexu, Imperial Commissioner".

On the patient card it says, "The Imperial Commissioner's health has improved since he was given the hernia band. The band around his stomach slips off when he coughs. According to his description of his symptoms he seems to have asthma as well. I sent him some medicine for it. To thank me he later sent some fruits and other gifts."

After Lin Zexu had the confiscated opium destroyed at Humen, almost all the British retreated to Hong Kong and Macao. So when the Americans requested resumption of trade, Lin Zexu approved their request swiftly so that Dr. Parker's hospital could continue its business. More and more people in Guangzhou learned about the effectiveness of Western medication and came for the treatment of their diseases. The in-patient wards were soon filled with patients from all over. Lin Zexu paid a special inspection visit to the hospital where Dr. Parker was called in to meet him. Lin said to him, "I wanted to ask you to come up with a prescription for those addicted to opium." Dr. Parker had seen the agony and suffering of those who smoked opium. He experimented on ways to relieve their pain, which proved to be fairly effective. This made Lin Zexu even more awed by the miracles of western medicine and more keen to acquire Western knowledge.

This is where Lin Zexu differed from other officials in the Qing Court.

Having realized the insufficiency of his knowledge, Lin Zexu was attentive to information worth collecting when he dealt with the foreigners, so as to make up for what he lacked, and broaden his thinking. This was his main method for understanding and studying the outside world.

After successfully destroying the opium at Humen, Lin Zexu knew that the British colonialists would definitely return for revenge. To prepare for the continued struggles to come, it was imperative to study the "barbarian sentiment", particularly the attitudes and trends of the British.

In a bid to learn and study the "barbarian sentiment", Lin Zexu hired people to translate Western newspapers and books in his commissioner's office. This effort lasted two years, until Lin Zexu was removed from his position by the Qing Court. Since he did not speak English, Lin Zexu kept people who were good at translation, and appointed them to important positions. At Lin's request, the personnel translated the relevant content in the *Macao Newspaper,* reprinted by the *Guangzhou Weekly Newspaper* being run by the British merchants. They classified different types of information and compiled the Chinese translation into a *Macao Monthly* for Lin Zexu's reference. He would include information of importance into his memorials to be submitted to Emperor Daoguang.

To investigate foreign information directly, Lin Zexu also began to study English words by heart. He once inquired of the British about the situation in the UK and Turkey. He also talked to the British and Bengalee to learn more about the plantation, production, classification and pricing of opium. Having the courage to learn a "barbarian language" was rare among the provincial governors in the Qing government.

Lin's desire to learn made the "foreign barbarians sell English books to the Chinese in order to please him." He then ordered that relevant commentaries about China in the foreign press and periodicals be translated into Chinese and edited into a book, known as *Barbarian Words about Chinese Matters (Hua Shi Yi Yan)*. American congregational missionary Samuel R. Brown gave Lin Zexu the most updated political and geographical book of the time—*Cyclopedia of Geography,* published by Englishman Hugh Murray in 1836. Lin cherished it very much and ordered that it be translated swiftly. The Chinese translation was named *A Record of Four Continents (Si Zhou Zhi)*. The Chinese learned for the first time that the world was very large and there were many countries, including Britain, France, Portugal and Spain.

At the same time, Lin Zexu also paid attention to learning the rules for international intercourse to better deal with foreign countries. He edited *Laws of Various Countries (Ge Guo Lü Li)* based on the abridged translation of an authoritative publication on international laws in modern Europe, *Laws of Nations (Le droit des gens),* published by the Swiss Mr. Vattel in 1758. It became the earliest Chinese translation of international laws, a quarter century earlier than the translated book *Law of Nations (Wan Guo Gong Fa)* written by the American missionary William Alexander Parsons Martin (from *Elements of International Law*) in 1864.

It was a pity that such an open minded politician as Lin Zexu had to become a victim of the decadent politics of the late Qing Dynasty. When Lin was to set out for Xinjiang after being removed from his position, his good friend Wei Yuan learned the news and came to see him off. Following a long overnight conversation, Lin gave Wei Yuan some of the materials about foreign countries he had collected and translated during his time in Guangzhou, as well as the script of *A Record of Four Continents* (*Si Zhou Zhi*), entrusting him to compile a book based on these materials. The script would systematically introduce various nations of the world in a relatively short period of time, so as to help the Chinese people broaden their vision and understand the world.

Lin Zexu thus became the first to "open his eyes to observe the world" in the early modern history of China. Mao Zedong spoke highly of Lin, saying, "Our democratic revolution is to tear off the skins of imperialism, feudalism and bureaucratic-capitalism. Starting from Lin Zexu, we have been carrying out our revolution for over a century." He put Lin Zexu in the position of a forerunner of China's democratic revolutions. The current Premier of China, Wen Jiabao quoted Lin's poem in his first press conference as premier shortly after taking up the post, "I devote my life and death to the benefit of the nation. How can I pursue or avoid responsibilities just for personal fortune or trouble?"

Wei Yuan himself had the idea of compiling such a book and accepted Lin's request right away. After that, Wei carefully studied *A Record of Four Continents* (*Si Zhou Zhi*) and other materials translated from foreign publications. He also consolidated history books of dynasties, foreign maps, books he had collected himself and those which his friends had given, as well as the latest books by foreign missionaries, in order to supplement the material that Lin did not have. After over a year, Wei Yuan completed his 50-volume book, *Illustrated Treatise on the Maritime Kingdoms* (*Hai Guo Tu Zhi*), in December 1842. This book uses Lin's *A Record of Four Continents* (*Si Zhou Zhi*) as basic material but is more complete and systematic. *Illustrated Treatise on the Maritime Kingdoms* (*Hai*

Guo Tu Zhi), has more than 570,000 characters, while *A Record of Four Continents* (*Si Zhou Zhi*) has only 80,000. It was warmly received by the general public and became quite popular for some time. *Illustrated Treatise on the Maritime Kingdoms* (*Hai Guo Tu Zhi*) is regarded as the original work contributing to China's efforts in understanding the world.

Wei Yuan improved on this book several times. It was expanded to 60 volumes, 600,000 characters from the original 50 volumes in 1847 (the 27th year of Emperor Daoguang's reign). It was also supplemented with general introductions of the nations. In 1852, Wei took a study trip to Macao and Hong Kong, to obtain more material, which led to a further expansion in the new edition of *Illustrated Treatise on the Maritime Kingdoms* (*Hai Guo Tu Zhi*)—to 100 volumes with 880,000 characters. The documentation on the Opium War and the translated foreign press material, including the *Macao Monthly,* that Lin Zexu had given him, were all used and consolidated with notes of "original European compilation", "translated by official Lin Zexu" and "reedited by Wei Yuan" respectively.

Hard work as it was, Wei Yuan finally accomplished what Lin Zexu had entrusted him to do, while expounding his thinking of "learning from the barbarians". In explaining the purpose of compiling *Illustrated Treatise on the Maritime Kingdoms* (*Hai Guo Tu Zhi*) he said, "Why did I compile the book? I did it for using barbarians to fight against the barbarians, for engaging barbarians to negotiate with barbarians, for learning their superior techniques to contain them."

"Learning the superior techniques of the barbarians in order to contain the barbarians" was a brand new theme in the development of early modern Chinese thought. "Learning from the barbarians" is meant to imply learning from the West, which is a rather ordinary initiative to today's Chinese, and which nobody disputes. However, during Wei Yuan's time, it was quite a radical view. Wei Yuan believed that though the Americans and Europeans were called "barbarians", they differed widely from the aboriginal "barbarians" in Chinese history. They "clearly understand rites and morality, have mastered astronomy and geography, know physics thoroughly and are well versed with history". They are "extraordinary people" under the sun and "good friends" in the domain. They were worth learning from. Wei Yuan also criticized those who insisted on the traditional belief that "the Chinese are superior to barbarians" and opposed to "learning from the barbarians". He regarded these ignorant and boastful people as having limited scope and outlook, coupled with blind belief.

Based on critical thinking regarding the Opium War defeat, Wei Yuan pointed out that "the superior techniques of the barbarians" could be found in three areas: the first was warships; second, gunnery; and third, the methods for maintaining and training troops.

According to his understanding of the West, Wei made a relatively detailed account of Western "techniques and crafts" which most of the Chinese people had not seen or heard of at that time. To some benighted and ignorant bureaucrats and officials who were hard-line conservatives, the "superior techniques" Wei Yuan introduced were "extraordinary crafts and excessive skills" that ought not to be learned. Once learnt, they said it would sap a person's spirit and ambition, as well as blunt his determination. And the entire social morality would also become rotten and decadent.

To this Wei Yuan offered counter criticism. He pointed out the Russian example, saying, "The Russian emperor Peter the Great is a smart person. He found that the Russian techniques could not compete with the Western ones, so he traveled to western dockyards and arsenals to learn their advanced techniques. He then came back to Russia and taught his own nationals how to make machines. As a result, the machines they made surpassed those made in the Western countries. Russia thereafter became one of the great powers of Europe."

The Western machines always worked with the help of wind, water, and fire and its workers tried their best and racked their minds to produce machines for the people. He especially emphasized that "learning from the barbarians" should be done as soon as possible, because "only by acting swiftly could one not miss hard won opportunities", and when an opportunity is neglected, it never comes back. Therefore, learning from the barbarians was a time-bound imperative. He advocated hiring technicians from France, America, Portugal, etc., and learning techniques from them so that "we can turn their superior techniques into ours." Finally, he said, the Chinese should work hard in a down-to-earth manner; although China was defeated in the Opium War, as long as the Chinese people strive for progress with determination and keep their spirits high, China would definitely be able to turn the situation around with "the new wisdom", and emerge from the East as rich and strong as the nations in the West.

Wei Yuan's thoughts of "learning superior techniques from the barbarians" and his advocacy for reform had great influence on subsequent times. Chinese reformist leader Kang Youwei read Wei's *Illustrated Treatise on the Maritime Kingdoms* (*Hai Guo Tu Zhi*). Kang "read the book again at the age of 22 and regarded the book together with other Western learning materials as the basis for studying the Western world". Kang's student Liang Qichao also said, "Wei Yuan is actually the forerunner in studying and exploring foreign geography." Like Lin Zexu, Wei Yuan began a fresh trend and was a progressive figure in early modern Chinese history.

2. Empress Dowager Cixi Snuffs Out Reform

The "Sino-British Treaty of Nanjing" was signed and Emperor Daoguang felt much saddened by the news. The official historical record of Qing Dynasty reveals, "His Majesty bowed his head against the stairs of the palace after he returned from attending state affairs at the court. For an entire day and night he did not rest. The waiters could only hear him heaving deep sighs. When the drum hit the fifth time at dawn, His Majesty stamped hard on his feet and gave out a long sigh." After the defeat in the Opium War, Emperor Daoguang should have drawn a lesson and worked harder to advance reform aimed at strengthening the country. However, he did not adopt any measures for reform or innovation, except for taking to wearing patched trousers to show his frugality. Being penny-wise and pound-foolish, Emperor Daoguang remained in gloom for the rest of his life until his death.

The biggest dream of Emperor Daoguang's son and successor —Emperor Xianfeng—was to avenge the insult. However, the destiny of the state doomed it to be a dream he would never be able to realize. In September 1860, Emperor Xianfeng declared war against the British and the French, only to find the allied Angelo-French forces conquering Beijing, where they looted and burnt down the imperial Garden of Perfection and Brightness (Yuan-mingyuan, or the Old Summer Palace), popularly known as the "Garden of Gardens". Emperor Xianfeng died during his escape from Beijing.

In view of the repeated defeats and insults by the foreign powers, some knowledgeable members of the ruling elite in the Qing Court proclaimed, "China is now faced with changing circumstances and strong enemies, unprecedented for the past three thousand years." They inherited the thinking of "learning superior techniques from the barbarians" from Lin Zexu and Wei Yuan, who had studied and introduced China to advanced science and technologies. They built the modern civil and military industries and carried out reform activities in the areas of defense, diplomacy and education. These people are commonly known as the "Western affairs faction". They wished to save the Qing Dynasty by learning from the West and through the Westernization Movement aimed at seeking strength and wealth.

In the Cedar Hill cemetery outside the capital city of Hartford, in the US state of Connecticut, lies the resting place of a Chinese named Yung Wing (Rong Hong). It was he who brought 120 Chinese youngsters to the United States for extended overseas study in 1872. This was the first batch of government-sponsored overseas education missions by the Qing government. Yung Wing was considered the "father of Chinese students who study overseas".

Yung Wing was born in Zhuhai, Guangdong Province. In 1835, Yung Wing turned seven, but his family could not afford his education. His father worked in Macao, where he found that Robert Morrison's missionary boarding school provided education

Yung Wing

free of charge, and sent his son there to study. The school's principal and missionary teacher was Dr. Samuel Robbins Brown. Yung distinguished himself as a bright student with considerable initiative. In 1847, Dr. Brown went back to the United States due to health reasons, and took Yung and other Chinese students back with him to complete their secondary education in America. With Dr. Brown's support, Yung entered Yale University, and went on to become its first Chinese graduate. With the growing strength of the US and decay of the Qing Dynasty, an idea struck Yung Wing: "I was determined that China's forthcoming generation should enjoy the same educational advantages I had; that through Western education, China might be regenerated, and become enlightened and powerful." This became his "overseas education scheme", to which he devoted his life. In November 1854, Yung Wing politely declined invitations to stay on in the US, and returned to China to advocate sending students to study abroad.

After seven or eight years of effort, Yung Wing earned a reputation that won the appreciation and trust of some "Western affairs faction" bureaucrats. Once, when he was invited to help with the purchase of some machinery, Yung took advantage of his close contacts with the senior officials, to put forward his overseas education scheme, which was subsequently endorsed and approved by them. The jointly-signed memorial to apply for government support was finally approved by the Qing government in 1872. It had taken nearly 20 years of endeavor for him to turn his dream into reality.

The Qing government drafted a plan to send 120 students to America to study science, technology and engineering, urgently needed for advancing the Western-ization Movement. Considering the language barrier, 120 students aged between 10 and 15 years were to be selected for aptitude and character, and sent to the US in batches of 30 per year, for a duration of 15 years. All educational and living expenses were to be paid for by the government.

Zhan Tianyou (left), who later made great contribu-tions to the development of China's railways, with classmate Pan Mingzhong during the period of their studies in the United States

Despite the generous terms of the offer, there was little interest among the wealthier families from the capital and main cities in China. This was probably owing to the entrenched prejudice against foreign countries. Many people thought the US was a remote land of wilderness where people could strip off the skins of the Chinese people. Also, for parents it was hard to accept the

15-year commitment and separation from their children. Despite Yung's efforts, he could not get enough students. To fill the quota, Yung Wing personally went on recruitment drives to Guangdong Province, and even to Hong Kong; he traveled especially to the coastal communities, from where the Chinese had traditionally emigrated overseas and where the population was more aware of the advantages of a Western education. In August 1872, the first batch of 30 boys departed from Shanghai for America. In the following three batches too, Yung encountered similar difficulties in recruiting students. But his hard work helped him to finally send 120 boys on the educational mission to the US.

The Qing government's intention behind sending youngsters to the US was to have the boys learn the advanced technologies of America, while maintaining Chinese traditions in terms of thoughts—just like "old bottles filled with new wine". But reality ran counter to its will. These teenagers were exposed to the colorful world of American society, received American education and lived the American lifestyle, and every aspect of theirs became "Americanized". As time passed, they appeared less and less Chinese and acquired a great variety of American traits. Some started abandoning Chinese clothing and took to dressing up in American styles. The pigtails they wore were their mark of being Qing citizens. But the boys often got curious looks for the pigtails so some decided to have them shaved off, getting fake pigtails stuck on when they met officers from the Qing Court. As everyone knows, the pigtails were not simply about decoration and dressing at that time in China. They mattered politically—the proof of a person being loyal to the Qing Court. When officials uncovered the pigtail-shaving incidents, they became furious and immediately reported the boys' disloyal misconduct back to the Qing Court. There were other boys who became influenced by

America's religious culture and converted to Christianity. Several of them privately formed an informal Christian organization called *Societas Condita Causa Augendarum Rerum Chinensium Christiana* (Society Founded for the Increase of Chinese Christianity). They also declared its purpose to be the conversion of the Chinese empire. They gradually lost interest in the doctrines of Confucius' teaching, in the Four Books (the four major Confucian classics: *The Great Learning*, *The Doctrine of the Mean*, *The Analects of Confucius* and *Mencius*) and the Five Classics (the *Book of Songs, the Book of History, the Book of Changes, the Book of Rites* and the *Spring and Autumn Annals*), held less admiration towards Confucius, and did not strictly abide by feudal proprieties or formalities. On the contrary, they became infatuated with individual rights, freedom and democracy. Some boys also began dating American girls. To Yung, who had been nurtured in American culture, these changes were only natural. However, to the officials of the Qing Court, this was an intolerable sign of forgetting their origins.

Also, the Qing government had only limited trust in Yung Wing, and had appointed him as the associate commissioner of the Chinese Educational Mission, while installing another less competent and conservative official as the commissioner. They often disagreed with each other on matters relating to the education of the young students. The commissioner frequently wrote

Some children who were sent to the United States for study became Westernized.

memorials to the Court, reporting on how the students had became Americanized, and how disobedient they were. He also reported how Yung Wing gave a loose hand to the boys and breached his duty, highlighting his "arrogance" while casting the students in the worst light; he accused Yung of indulging their neglect of Chinese studies and their adoption of foreign ways. Yung Wing, who was not good at politics, never thought of writing memorials to the Court, or letters to the "Western affairs faction" bureaucrats to explain the situation. By and by, the Qing government lost political trust in the young students in the US. Eventually, an order came in August 1881 that all the young men return to China in three batches.

The news that the educational mission was being cancelled and the students were to return home shocked everyone, including Yung Wing, the students, and their teachers. In fact, Yale President Nolan Porter joined several other American friends in writing to the Qing Court to point out the mistake and to demand correction. The letter read: "All the young students your country has dispatched use their time well in developing their studies and research. They exhibit excellent performances in almost every subject. Their morality is also graceful and noble. They deserve to be the representatives of your great nation, so much that they have earned honors for your country. Young as they are, they are all keenly aware that every move and action of theirs matters in terms of the honor of their motherland, and they are all prudent and careful with their words and actions, beyond even grownups. Their fine behavior has achieved a very positive effect in that the prejudice held by few ignorant Americans is being gradually washed away. The feelings of Americans towards China are improving and are becoming increasingly harmonious. We feel incomparable regret in learning that the students have been recalled. To the boys, this moment is critical. The efforts of the past would be wasted, should they cut short their studies and return home. They are just like the bright flowers and ripened fruits of the roots and stems of young trees that have been slowly reared under patient watering and tillage."

The American media also followed the development closely. The *New York Times* carried a report on July 15, 1881, saying: "Evidence shows that the promising Chinese Educational Mission in the US is facing an abrupt termination…it would be a great pity if such a project is abandoned without due consideration…these youngsters, selected from outstanding families in China, have demonstrated gifted talent. They are liked everywhere they go." A commentary in *New York Times* on July 16 said, "The reason for which the scheme is being terminated isn't a secret. It is because the Chinese officials are concerned that these youth, without strict traditional education, will not be able to truly help their own country. No matter what prompted the Chinese government to start this overseas education mission, it is sure that the vision with which the government sees this cause is far more myopic than that of Dr. Yung Wing's."

However, despite these comments, the stubborn and decaying Qing government did not change its stance for the sake of main-taining the stability of its rule. Yung Wing's overseas education scheme was aborted and the Qing Empire's dream of strength-ening itself through overseas-educated students, shattered.

Kang Youwei

But the stability the Qing Court had become increasingly hard to maintain, and internal changes were becoming ever more ubiquitous.

In 1882, a Cantonese named Kang Youwei went to Beijing for a civil service exam. While passing through Shanghai, he bought a lot of Western books and newspapers, including the

Review of the Times (Wan Guo Gong Bao) by Young John Allen. Kang Youwei was deeply inspired by an article in the periodical on foot binding. *Review of the Times* had been publishing numerous articles to persuade Chinese women not to bind their feet, elaborating the physiological and orthopedic harm it does to the body. Binding women's feet into a "three-inch gold lotus" (known as San Cun Jin Lian) is an undesirable custom inherited since the Song Dynasty (960-1279). Foot-binding at an early age required that the bones of their toes be broken for twisting the shape of their feet, to make them look small. The smaller, the prettier. Women suffered a lot in foot binding. It was popularly said that if a girl bound her feet into three-inch gold lotuses, she would shed enough tears to fill a jar. In the past 1,000 years, women's bound feet became the primary aspect of evaluating their beauty instead of their appearance, and people even complimented them in lyrics and poems. In a foreign postcard of the late Qing Dynasty, foreigners compared Chinese women's feet and hands, and were surprised that their feet were smaller than their hands.

After returning to his hometown, Kang Youwei created the "Community of Anti-Foot Binding", together with some other liberal gentlemen. He started challenging the undesirable custom that was harming women's health, and even unbound his daughter's and niece's feet. He and his student Liang Qichao also wrote an article about it in order to build a momentum for foot unbinding. Inspired by them, several cities established an "Unbound Foot Community", which had great impact on society. In order to influence the common people, the communities wrote a huge amount of street poetry, such as: "Who is the woman with a pair of small feet which are three-inches long? She may be afraid of being blown away by the wind, because her feet are too small to support her body. It must feel as difficult as walking 10,000 miles."

"Mum and Dad bound her feet when she was five or six years old. She cried late in the night because of the pain in her feet, but her mother would hear none of it."

Kang Youwei especially emphasized linking unbound feet to the strengthening of the country and the optimizing of the race: "Unbinding women's feet is the starting point of independence, and the origin of race-strengthening. By improving women's physical condition, they will be able to climb high mountains and achieve the goals they want; they will become strong as men; they will learn at school and cultivate the spirit of patriotism; they will be able to do exercises, improve their health and give birth to healthy babies. Only in this way, can we save our country from outside danger." Kang Youwei's radical opinions made him outstanding among the people of his time and he became a pioneer of his era.

At this time, Emperor Guangxu was simply a nominal head, while the Qing Dynasty was actually being controlled by Empress Dowager Cixi. Cixi was very calculating and had a strong desire for power. She was originally a concubine of Emperor Xianfeng and had gained the position of empress dowager by doing whatever it took. She lacked the capability to rule a country, but was very good at satisfying her personal interests through the misuse of her powers, which made the Westernization Movement difficult to implement.

In 1888, the bureaucrats from the "Western affairs faction" established the Beiyang Fleet, which was then at the same level of competence as China's peer nations. However, the day the Beiyang Fleet was established was also the beginning of its decline, since it did not purchase any new vessels subsequently due to lack of funding. The fleet soon became outdated. After 1891, it even stopped purchasing gunnery and munitions, because the military fund was diverted to renovate Cixi's Summer Palace. This directly led to the defeat of the Beiyang Fleet in the First Sino-Japanese War (1894-1895). In 1895, the Qing government was forced to sign the Treaty of Shimonoseki, ceding land and paying indemnities to Japan.

At precisely the time the Treaty of Shimonoseki was signed, in April 1895, the national examination to the highest imperial posts had concluded and the candidates were awaiting the results in Jingshi (Beijing). When they heard that the Qing government had ceded Taiwan and Liaodong (the eastern and southern part of Liaoning Province) and paid 200 million *liang* (10 million kg.) of silver to Japan, they were frustrated. Those from Taiwan shed bitter tears. Kang Youwei and his student Liang Qichao were among this group. On April 22, Kang Youwei and Liang Qichao wrote a memorial of 18,000 characters named "Petition Letter to the Emperor". In their appeal, signed by 1,200 candidates from 18 provinces, they expressed concern over the dangerous situation China was in. On May 2, led by Kang and Liang, the candidates,

The Treaty of Shimonoseki, signed by China and

along with thousands of citizens, gathered in front of the gate of the Court of Censors, to present the letter they had written to the Emperor. As the candidates used to commute by public vehicles, this petition was called the "Public Vehicle Petition".

The "Public Vehicle Petition" symbolizes the emergence of reformists in modern China's history. The "Public Vehicle Petition" warned of the serious outcomes of the "Treaty of Shimonoseki" and suggested four measures to combat them: 1. Send out an imperial edict to encourage the common people; 2. Move the capital to Shanghai; 3. Modernize the Qing Imperial Army; 4. Implement reforms. Kang said that the first three suggestions were to deal with the enemy and the fourth one was aimed toward nation building.

With the obstinate bureaucrats standing in the way, the memorial was unable to reach Emperor Guangxu. However, the content of the memorial spread and shocked everybody in the capital. Thanks to the "Public Vehicle Petition", Kang Youwei and Liang Qichao obtained leadership status in the innovation and reform movement.

On the second day of the "Public Vehicle Petition" agitation, the results of the national examination were declared. Kang Youwei was successful and was awarded the position of the director of the Department of Works. Soon, Kang Youwei sent another memorial to Emperor Guangxu, advocating the establishing of chambers as soon as possible. He believed that there were several things that needed to be done first: 1. Issue imperial edicts to encourage the common people to give advice on national policies; 2. Invite persons of insight to discuss affairs of the state; 3. Establish a consulting department for the emperor; 4. Establish a newspaper publishing house; 5. Establish organizations specialized in employing talent to work in the government. However, officials in the Court of Censors refused to submit the memorial to the emperor on his behalf, stating that since he was in the Department of Works, his memorial should be submitted by his own department. He turned to the Department of Works but was refused there too. Moreover, it was impossible for the Department of War to submit the memorial for him, because the head of that department Rong Lu was a confidant of Empress Dowager Cixi. However, Kang did not give up and went to ask Weng Tonghe—Emperor Guangxu's teacher and a minister in the Department of Revenue—for help. Weng was supportive of the innovation movement. After talking with Kang, Weng spoke highly of Kang's and his followers' ideas.

In August 1895 Kang Youwei established newspapers to promote reformist ideas. Under his leadership, lots of magazines and newspapers, and different kinds of political groups advocating reform and innovation, appeared. Among them, the Society for Study of National Strengthening, established by Kang and Liang, was the most influential and was supported by senior officials like Weng Tonghe. Within the following two years, the number of societies, academies and newspaper publishing houses nationwide surpassed 50. The establishment of publishing houses and the societies played a supportive role in the innovation movement and widened its influence.

The development of the political reform movement created fear among the obstinate bureaucrats of the feudal ruling classes. They stigmatized and assaulted the reformers. The reformers carried out fierce debates with them. The debates were mainly focused on: whether to carry out the reforms; whether to promote civil rights and implement constitutional monarchy; and whether to advocate learning from the West and reform the educational system. The debate made some intellectuals give up their feudal mindset and push the reform movement forward.

In November 1897, Germany occupied Jiaozhou Bay off the coast of Shandong Province, which angered the nation. In December, Kang Youwei wrote another memorial to the emperor, stating that the great Western powers were eating into China and the country was in imminent danger. He posed three counter policies: 1. Decide the policies yourself and make an announcement to reform as Peter the Great and the Japanese emperor Meiji did; 2. Invite talented officials to plan the reforms; 3. Urge the provincial ministers to implement the new policies. He emphasized that the first suggestion was the best option and could strengthen the power of the country; the second suggestion was an intermediate measure, which could help the country maintain its current position; and the third suggestion was the worst, which could only prevent the country from being conquered.

This memorial was published by all provincial newspapers and spread all across the country. Weng Tonghe made good use of this and asked Emperor Guangxu to summon Kang Youwei to an interview. Since officials in the Qing Dynasty ranked lower than the fourth grade were not allowed to meet the emperor in person, Emperor Guangxu told his ministers, Weng Tonghe, Rong Lu and several others, to invite Kang to answer their questions.

The conservative bureaucrat Rong Lu said to Kang: "The laws set by our ancestors cannot be changed." Kang replied: "The land of our ancestors cannot even be defended, and you are talking about the laws of the ancestors?" Weng Tonghe was wary of Kang's words raising the hackles of the conservatives and asked Kang: "How will you get the funds for reform?" Kang answered: "The Japanese banks issue paper notes, the French government exempts stamp tax and the Indian government collects tax on farming to raise revenue. As long as we change the system, tax revenue can be increased 10-fold."

Weng Tonghe reported this conversation to the emperor. Guangxu issued an edict that Kang Youwei's memorials and letters be presented to him and barred any kind of obstruction.

1898 is the year of Wuxu in the Chinese lunar calendar. On January 29 of this year, Kang Youwei sent a memorial to the emperor known as the *Memorial for Outlining the Overall Program in Response to the Imperial Edict.* He laid down three fundamentals: 1. Summon all the ministers to the Qianqing Gate to make them take an oath to reform; 2. Establish a department for submitting the memorials; 3. Establish a system to regulate the Qing Court and to make and implement rules. This memorial could be regarded as the guiding principle of the reforms. Kang also presented to the emperor several books, such as the Japanese *Meiji Reform* and the Russian *Peter the Great Reform* written by himself. He pointed out in his books that the system of the European and American countries had been established after almost 300 years of their foundation. Japan learned from the Western countries and 30 years after that, it achieved its success. If China learned from Japan, its systems could become effective in three years; in five years, everything could run in the right orbit; in eight years, great achievements could be made; and in 10 years, China could become one of the great powers in the world.

In the spring of 1898, another national examination was held. Kang wanted to capitalize on this opportunity where candidates were gathering in Beijing, to build up such a momentum as to make reform inevitable. On April 12, Kang established the Society for the Preservation of the Nation (Bao Guo Hui). In its first conference, two to three hundred people attended Kang's speech. In the second conference on April 15, Liang Qichao came to make a speech. In the following conference, the reform movement was pushed to its climax by the participation of scholar-bureaucrats.

Encouraged by these events, Emperor Guangxu made up his mind to carry out the reforms. He wanted to gain actual control of the military and political power of the country and become the real emperor. This is because he was only four years old when he ascended the throne, and Empress Dowager Cixi was the one who had since ruled behind the scenes. In 1889, when Guangxu got married, although Cixi had told Guangxu to take over the affairs of the state, in reality the power was still in her hands. At the same time, Emperor Guangxu also wanted to reform the administration of the officials in order to save the Qing Dynasty from imminent danger. He decided to express his resolve in implementing the reforms.

In a meeting with Cixi, Emperor Guangxu told her about the general content of the "Public Vehicle Petition" and stated his own new political plans. To his surprise, Cixi did not oppose his ideas and said: "As long as it does not breach the ancestors' system, you can decide on your own." Therefore, under the encouragement of the reformist bureaucrats and intellectuals, Emperor Guangxu issued an "Imperial Edict Clarifying State Affairs", declaring the reform program, on June 11, 1898.

On June 16th, Emperor Guangxu summoned Kang Youwei for an interview, which Kang Youwei had dreamed of for long. Kang had a two-hour conversation with the emperor.

Kang asked the emperor to implement the reforms with the overall picture in mind, and to "reform the laws first". Emperor Guangxu agreed. Kang then asked the emperor: "If your majesty agrees to the reforms, why don't you carry them out instead of sitting idle?" The emperor, afraid of being overheard, inspected the window, and then sighed: "I have no choice!" Kang realized that this was an allusion to Cixi and Rong Lu. However, he encouraged

Empress Dowager Cixi

Emperor Guangxu to use his powers and carry out the reforms to the best of his capacity. He suggested that it was unnecessary to make all the old ministers resign from their offices. Instead, he could guarantee their high posts and salaries; meanwhile, the emperor could promote talented reformers and send them to implement the new policies. Only in this way could the obstacles be reduced.

After this conversation, Emperor Guangxu could have promoted Kang Youwei and put him into important positions. But due to the opposition of Rong Lu and some others, and for fear of irritating Empress Dowager Cixi, Emperor Guangxu appointed Kang to a relatively low position, but also allowed him to send memorials directly. Kang took advantage of this privilege and constantly sent memorials to the emperor and made suggestions regarding the affairs of the state. Through the approval of Emperor Guangxu, these memorials and memorandums resulted in over 110 edicts and orders.

The main content of the imperial edicts and orders issued by Emperor Guangxu includes: Economically, establish an agricultural and industrial bureau, and a road and mine bureau; advocate establishing of businesses; build railways and mines; organize a chamber of commerce; and carry out reforms on finance. Politically, broaden channels of communication and allow the common people to send memorials to the emperor; reduce the old army and organize new armies. Culturally, abandon the stereotyped writing and advocate learning from the West; establish the Metropolitan university (predecessor of Peking University); establish bureaus of book translation and send students to study abroad; and reward those who contribute to scientific innovations and books. The aims of these edicts lay in learning from Western culture, their scientific technologies and management systems, and developing capitalism and establishing institutional monarchy to strengthen the powers of China.

After the reforms were carried out, the conservatives could tolerate it no longer. The officials in most provinces were suspicious and skeptical about the new policies. They all performed their duties in a perfunctory manner and in fact did not carry out the new policies. Most of the edicts thus became nullified. Some even sent memorials to Empress Dowager Cixi, asking her to rule behind the scenes once again and sentence Kang Youwei and Liang Qichao to death. Rumors had it that Empress Dowager Cixi would dethrone Emperor Guangxu and install another emperor. The Chinese nationals were disquieted, not knowing the future of the country.

Emperor Guangxu decided to take preemptive action. In September, he secretly summoned the reformists to discuss counter measures. Kang believed that seizing control over the military was the top priority. The militarily powerful Yuan Shikai, who commanded the New Army, had once joined the Society for Study of National Strengthening and was inclined toward the reforms. They decided to appeal to him to protect Emperor Guangxu and to eliminate Cixi's die-hard followers and Rong Lu, Governor of Zhili Province. Yuan Shikai however played both sides: while on one hand he told Emperor Guangxu that "killing Rong Lu is like killing a dog", on the other, he sent messages to Rong Lu in Tianjin. He also went to Beijing at night to report to Cixi. According to normal practice, Guangxu was required to go to the Summer Palace to wish good health to Cixi on September 20. However, Cixi suddenly appeared in the Forbidden City in the afternoon of September 19. Emperor Guangxu knew

Liang Qichao

that his plan had failed due to an information leak. He was quite frightened, knowing he did not command the military troops. The next day, Empress Dowager Cixi published an imperial edict in the name of Emperor Guangxu, "Due to health reasons, Emperor Guangxu asks Empress Dowager Cixi to come back for 'regency'." Cixi then put Emperor Guangxu under house arrest. The short reform of only 103 days was thus pulled down. This short-lived reform movement is referred to in Chinese history as "Hundred Days' Reform" or "Reform Movement of 1898".

Subsequently, Empress Dowager Cixi ordered the arrest and execution of Kang Youwei, Liang Qichao and others. Luckily, the emperor had handed down a confidential edict, telling them to escape and hide as quickly as possible, prior to his being house arrested. Upon receipt of the edict, Kang swiftly departed on a British commercial ship from Tianjin to Shanghai, where he transferred further to Hong Kong. Liang rushed to the Japanese Legation seeking refuge, and got a chance to get himself to Yokohama, Japan. All the new policies were abolished, except for the Metropolitan University.

The Hundred Days' Reform by the Qing government to seek strengthening through reform had failed completely.

3. The Success of Sun Yat-sen

The failure of the Hundred Days' Reform shattered the dream of the Chinese who were relying on the Qing government to carry out reform and strengthen the country. After that, the revolution led by Sun Yat-sen takes center stage in Chinese history.

Sun Yat-sen, also known as Sun Wen or Sun Zhongshan, was born in 1866 in Cuiheng Village of Guangdong Province. Cuiheng Village was surrounded by the sea in three directions and mountains on the other, and had infertile soil. Many people lived off the sea and led bitter lives. Sun Yat-sen's family too was becoming poorer day by day. In 1879, the 13-year-old boy accompanied his mother to go to Honolulu to look for his elder brother. There he studied in a missionary school and started accepting Western education, which proved to be a turning point in his life. Sun Yat-sen thus had a broader vision than his fellow countrymen and was outstandingly knowledgeable. The cession of land and payment of indemnities aroused anti-Qing sentiments in Sun Yat-sen. He made many friends who shared this emotion and denounced the administration of

Sun Yat-sen

the Qing Court. They freely talked about the affairs of state and planned China's future.

In 1887, the 22-year-old Sun Yet-sen studied in Hong Kong College of Medicine for Chinese. The dean and surgery director James Cantline soon became familiar with Sun, because Sun always topped the class. When Cantline visited China's leprosy-affected regions, Sun accompanied him as an interpreter. They became more familiar with each other during this period.

In 1892, Sun graduated and earned his license for medical practice from the Hong Kong College of Medicine for Chinese. However, Sun Yat-sen did not want to become a doctor. In 1894, Sun established the anti-Qing government organization, Revive China Society, in Honolulu. After that, he returned to China to prepare for an armed uprising in Guangzhou. However, due to careless planning, information was leaked and the uprising was quelled midway.

From this uprising, the Qing government learned that Sun

Yat-sen was a dangerous figure and decided to arrest him at any cost. On one hand, they sent many spies to Hong Kong, Macao and Singapore to chase him and get him arrested; on the other, the Qing government informed the Chinese ministers working in Asia, America and Europe to keep an eye on him and arrest him when time allowed.

Sun first escaped from Guangdong to Hong Kong by a small boat. After arriving in Hong Kong, he went to meet his teacher, Cantline, and inquired about what to do next. Cantline introduced Sun to a lawyer, who suggested that he escape to other countries instead of staying in Hong Kong, where he could be arrested. Sun cut his hair short, changed his appearance further and escaped to Japan. Soon after his arrival in Japan, Sun went to Honolulu to raise money to prepare for a revolution.

In Honolulu, Sun happened to meet Cantline, and the two promised to meet in London. Sun planned to set off from Honolulu, halt at San Fransico and New York in order to raise money, and then go to Britain.

In September 1896, Sun set off from New York to London by boat and on September 30, he arrived in Liverpool, Britain. During this period, the legation of the Qing government in America heard about his imminent arrival in Britain and informed the legation in Britain about it. The legation in Britain immediately assigned detectives to track Sun.

After his arrival in London on October 1, Sun immediately went to visit Cantline. The Cantlines were very hospitable and arranged for Sun to stay in a hotel near their house. Thereafter, Sun visited them everyday and also Cantline's friend, Dr. Patrick Manson. Both warned Sun to be cautious of Chinese ministers, because Cantline's house was adjacent to the Chinese Legation. Sun, however, did not pay heed, and much to his surprise, he was arrested by the Chinese Legation several days later.

At half-past ten on October 11, while he was on his way to the Cantline's, Sun was cornered by three armed Chinese who had been keeping tabs on him. He was subsequently held in a small fenced room on the third floor of the legation's office. The Chinese ministers were trying to hire a 7,000-pound boat to transport him stealthily from Britain to China and then sentence him to death. Sun was eager to tell his teacher about his grave situation, and solicited the help of British workers in the legation to send letters for him, but failed.

At this critical point, Sun took advantage of Christian beliefs to convince a British servant, Cole, and Mrs. Howe, a chamberlain, to help him. He told them the story of the Turkish Sudan killing Armenian Christians, comparing the Chinese emperor to the Turkish Sudan. "I am a Christian. If I am sent back to China, I will be sentenced to death. Don't you have the heart to help me?" Finally, Sun won the sympathy of the two.

On October 17, Cole threw a letter into Cantline's house, which said, "Your friend was arrested on Sunday by the Chinese Legation. They want to send him back to China and then sentence him to death… If not rescued immediately, he will be executed." The next day, Cole brought two cards written by Sun Yat-sen to Cantline. The cards said: 1. I was arrested by the Chinese Legation and they will send me back to China and sentence me to death. Please rescue me as soon as possible; 2. Please take good care of this man who brings you the letter. He is very poor. In order to help me, he may lose his job; 3. The Chinese Legation has already hired a boat which will send me back to China. I am locked up and cannot contact anyone.

After learning about Sun's perilous situation, Cantline hurriedly turned to Scotland Yard for help and asked them to intervene in the matter. The next day, he and Dr. Patrick Manson went to the Ministry of Foreign Affairs and reported the illegal kidnapping of Sun Yat-sen by the Qing Legation in London. Even though the Ministry of Foreign Affairs promised to investigate, due to the complicated procedures of the administrative affairs, the matter could not be resolved immediately. Cantline also went to negotiate with the Qing Legation but received a cold reception. Mr. Cantline and Dr. Patrick Manson were extremely worried about Sun's situation and knew that if they could not rescue him immediately, the consequences would be too ghastly to contemplate. In order to gain more time, the two acted separately. Dr. Manson went to inform the Qing Legation that Sun Yat-sen's kidnapping was known to other people, and that the British government and the Scotland Yard would intervene in the matter; Cantline, meanwhile, drove to *The Times* and met with reporters. He told them about Sun's kidnapping by the Qing Legation in detail, but *The Times* was very cautious, as it did not want to become involved in an international imbroglio. In order to preempt the Qing Legation's actions, Cantline hired a private detective to sit in a car near the legation's gate to spy on their movements.

Cantline was desperate, and the last place he went to for help was the local courthouse. There he happened to meet a reporter of a tabloid named *Globe*. *Globe* was a small newspaper, and was eager to find something hot and explosive to report in order to promote its sales. The reporter promised Cantline that he would report the news with a shocking headline. On October 22, *Globe*'s headlines read: "Surprising News: Revolutionist Kidnapped and Detained in London". *Globe* was the first to reveal Sun Yat-sen's kidnapping in London. The media and politicians in Britain were stunned. Soon reporters from *Central Review* and *Daily Mail* gathered at Cantline's home and the Qing Legation to gather news and file reports.

As the news spread, the British citizens sympathetic toward China's revolution swarmed to the Qing Legation, and strongly objected to its illegal conduct. The British government had also intervened in the matter. Under pressure from all sides, the Qing Legation was forced to release Sun Yat-sen. On October 23, Cantline welcomed Sun as the latter was freed. When Sun walked out of the legation, the streets were crowded with people, as the Britons waved to this hero who was fighting against China's feudal administration. Sun took this opportunity to reveal the Qing government's plot to kidnap him and began propagating his revolutionary stand to the public. At the same time, the *New York Times, China Mail* (Hong Kong), *Current Affairs Daily* (Shanghai), etc. also reported Sun's escape from danger in London. From then on, westerners began to know of Sun Yat-sen and learned that he was the leader of China's democratic revolution.

After his release, Sun wrote letters to London's newspapers expressing his appreciation of the British government and the kind assistance from London's newspapers. At the request of many parties, in 1897 Sun wrote a book about his experiences in London and called the book *Kidnapped in London*, which made him further known all around the world. Sun said in his book that it was in London that he began to devote himself to state affairs. While mentioning Cantline, Sun wrote, "I was so touched by what he did for me that I shed tears." Thus the friendship between the two deepened.

Sun Yat-sen had had a narrow escape; and the revolution he had led turned the corner and entered a new stage. His influence on China's national revolution expanded widely and rapidly. He became the most widely recognized leader of the democratic revolution.

After his release, Sun stayed on in London for a while. He read many books in the British museum. Thus, based on the socialist thinking which was popular in Britain at that time, he conceived the rudiments of his signature principles of Nationalism, Democracy, and People's livelihood. He spared no effort in advocating revolutionary thoughts and organizing revolutionary activities among overseas Chinese students.

In 1905, on Sun Yat-sen's initiative the Revive China Society and other revolutionary societies united to establish the first national revolutionary organization, Chinese United League, with Sun as its premier. He posed the following political guidelines: "to drive away the Manchurians and restore China, to create the Republic and evenly distribute land rights". These political guidelines were summarized as "nationalism, democracy and the people's livelihood". With the propagation and mobilization of the revolutionary theories, the revolution that Sun Yat-sen led became more and more influential.

After several years of revolutionary struggle and 10 defeats, the Wuchang Uprising finally succeeded on October 10, 1911. The revolutionary army took over the city of Wuchang by night. The first capitalist local revolutionary regime in Chinese history—the Hubei Military Government of the Republic of China—was established on October 11, 1911, and abolished the title of the Qing emperor's reign.

Following the Wuchang uprising, the provinces in the South declared independence from the Qing Dynasty, establishing military governments one after another. The 1911 Revolution (1911 was the year of Xinhai in the Chinese lunar calendar) spread across the country. The Qing Dynasty quickly collapsed under the pressure of revolutions occurring simultaneously in a number of provinces.

Even though Sun Yat-sen himself did not participate in the Wuchang Uprising, he was elected the provisional president by representatives from all the provinces in the Southern Conferences, on January 1, 1912. This was because of his reputation as a revolutionary. The Gregorian calendar was then adopted. Sun Yat-sen was sworn in as the provisional president in Nanjing and the Republic of China was officially established. The 1911 Revolution overturned the rule of the Qing Dynasty, which had lasted more than 260 years. It ended the three thousand years plus of autocratic monarchy in China and established a capitalist republic. Sun Yat-sen's revolution had succeeded.

At a time when the southern provinces had declared their loyalty to the Republic of China, the provinces in the north had yet to break away from the Qing government. Sun Yat-sen believed that ending the Qing government's rule was the true measure of success of the revolution. After the revolution, he believed a benev-

On March 10, 1912, Yuan Shikai (center, standing) became the Republic of China's first president.

olent era of political democracy and industrial prosperity would emerge. As long as the Qing government was overturned and the revolutionary objectives accomplished, it did not matter to him who became the president. Though the representatives from southern provinces had elected Sun Yat-sen as provisional president, the president's post was in fact awaiting Yuan Shikai, who held formidable military power in Beijing (he commanded the majority of the former Qing Army). Soon, the South began to negotiate with the North. In order to win over the Chinese people in the north, Sun Yat-sen voluntarily offered the position of president to Yuan Shikai after Yuan had agreed to join the Republic, even though he did not completely trust Yuan. After becoming the president, Yuan Shikai moved the capital to Beijing, which directly caused the restoration of monarchy and the ensuing conflicts between the warlords. The famous writer Lu Xun once commented on Sun Yat-sen's revolution as follows: the 1911 Revolution only cut off the pigtails. The old ruling elite turned themselves into revolutionaries all of a sudden, and became mandarins with new titles.

Even though Sun Yet-sen's revolution was not thorough, he devoted his life to overthrowing the Qing Dynasty and rejuvenating China. Because of this, he won worldwide admiration and was respected by all Chinese as the Father of the Republic, the only revolutionary respected on both the mainland and Taiwan. Mao Zedong called Sun Yet-sen "a great Chinese revolutionist and our predecessor". He also said, "We should have a clear head to hold up the banner of Sun Yat-sen's; this is what we should hold on to until we die, and even upon our death we should pass it on to our sons and grandsons." The Chinese Communist Party regards itself as the heir of Sun Yat-sen's revolutionary cause.

图书在版编目（CIP）数据

中国简史：从孔夫子到邓小平．上：英文／谢春涛主编．
—北京：新世界出版社，2008.11
ISBN 978-7-80228-565-1

I. 中⋯ II. 谢⋯ III. 中国－历史－英文 IV. K20

中国版本图书馆 CIP 数据核字（2008）第 171388 号

China Through the Ages – from Confucius to Deng (Vol. I)
中国简史：从孔夫子到邓小平（上）

主　　编：谢春涛
作　者：刘阅斌　张　军　李庆钢　沈传亮
策　　划：林良旗　张海鸥
责任编辑：李淑娟
翻　译：周　钢　李　央　邬　安
英文审定：谭宏凯
封面设计：兆远书装
责任印制：李一鸣　黄厚清
出版发行：新世界出版社
社　　址：北京市西城区百万庄大街 24 号（100037）
总编室电话：＋ 86 10 6899 5424　　68326679（传真）
发行部电话：＋ 86 10 6899 5968　　68998705（传真）
本社中文网址：http://www.nwp.cn
本社英文网址：http://www.newworld-press.com
版权部电子信箱：frank@nwp.com.cn
版权部电话：＋ 86 10 6899 6306
印刷：北京外文印刷厂
经销：新华书店
开本：787 × 1092　　1/16
字数：180 千字　　印张：16.5
版次：2009 年 1 月第 1 版　　2009 年 1 月北京第 1 次印刷
书号：ISBN 978-7-80228-565-1
定价：78.00 元